LIBERTY'S
A BIOGRAPHY OF A SHOP

Title-page

Original architect's drawing of the Great Marlborough Street elevation of Liberty's Tudor building by Edwin T. Hall and E. Stanley Hall.

Cover design

By Alastair N. Campbell, in original 'Peacock Feather' fabric design by Rex Silver, c. 1900.

By the same author

A Punch History of Manners and Modes, 1841–1940
Shops and Shopping, 1800–1914
View of Fashion
Women in Print – Writing Women and Women's Magazines, from the Restoration to the Accession of Victoria

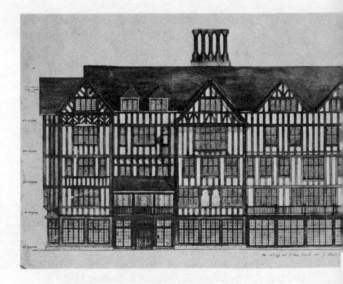

LIBERTY'S

A BIOGRAPHY OF A SHOP

ALISON ADBURGHAM

LONDON GEORGE ALLEN & UNWIN LTD

ISBN 0 04 380021 1 hardback

Printed in Great Britain
by Sir Joseph Causton and Sons Ltd

Typeset in 12 point Fournier type
by the Aldine Press, Letchworth, Herts

Reproduction by Maximum Litho Ltd

FOREWORD

'There is properly no history, only biography,' wrote Emerson; so I have called this history of Liberty's a biography of a shop. The life of its founder, of course, is inextricably interwoven with the conception, birth, and early growth of the shop; but the thing he created continues after him – a living, growing, changing personality in its own right, with its own character, quirks, obstinacies, and ambience. Many of its most endearing characteristics are inherited from the founder, passed down through his descendants who still guide the destiny of the shop. The young men who have overtaken each generation, adding their fresh impetus and influence, have included many who have come into Liberty's from outside the family. Some of these are named in this story, but many have had to be omitted – as indeed many of the family, too – or the book would have become a roll call.

A shop is part of the social history of its environment – in Liberty's case, of London. Its development is influenced by changes in social pressures, class patterns, governmental policies. It is affected by wars and depressions, by trade booms and enemy bombs, by changes in fashion and taste. What gives Liberty's its peculiar distinction is that it has not only reflected these changes, but has itself contributed to artistic movements and the development of fashionable taste. Arthur Lasenby Liberty told his artist and designer friends that, if he could only have a shop of his own, he would change the whole look of fashion in dress and interior decoration. He got his shop, and he did.

I wish to thank the present Chairman, Mr Arthur Stewart-Liberty, for all his kind help, also other members of his family. In particular I am grateful for the generous co-operation of Mr Hilary Blackmore in making available information to which I could not otherwise have had access, including personal recollections handed down to him by his father. To many present and past members of the staff I owe thanks for their help, most especially Mr Stanley M. Porter who, in his role as Liberty archivist, has given me invaluable assistance. I am indebted to Miss Elizabeth Aslin, Keeper of the Bethnal Green Museum, to Mrs Shirley Bury, Mrs Barbara Morris, and Mr David R. Coachworth of the Victoria & Albert Museum, to Miss Evelyn M. Jowett, Librarian of Merton and Morden, and to Mr K. Murphy, Librarian of *The Guardian*. My thanks are also due to Miss Nesta Llewellyn, and to Mr John Gloag.

Published books, magazines, and other sources directly quoted are

acknowledged in the text. The *Liberty Lamp*, monthly staff magazine of
Liberty & Co., has been a rewarding source of inside information although
it unfortunately ran for only seven years, from February 1925 to January
1932. I have not included a bibliography of general background reading as
the period of the Liberty story is too long, and its associated interests too
varied, for relevant books to be contained within a reasonably short list.

ALISON ADBURGHAM, 1975

CONTENTS

Site of Arthur Liberty's shop, next the George Inn, Chesham, now the George and Dragon

I

THE ORIENTAL WAREHOUSE
AND THE ARTISTS

Arthur Lasenby Liberty was born on August 13, 1843, in the small market town of Chesham in Buckinghamshire. His father, also named Arthur Liberty, had a draper's shop in the High Street, next to the George Inn. He had married Rebecca Lasenby, a farmer's daughter from the nearby village of Chartridge, whose family had lived there for generations. It was to these Chiltern grass roots that their eldest son, Arthur Lasenby Liberty, returned half a century later to become Lord of the Manor and Patron of the Living of The Lee, a landowner of some three thousand acres, with several farms, many cottages, an Elizabethan manor house, and a coat-of-arms. He became a County Councillor, High Sheriff of Buckinghamshire, Deputy Lieutenant of the County, Freeman of the City of London, and was knighted in recognition of his services to the applied and decorative arts of the country. He gave The Lee village a green, built cottages, planted woods and avenues of trees, restored and extended the church, and finally became the first occupant of a Liberty family grave in the churchyard, leaving a handsome fortune and a world famous London department store.

His was a classic 'local boy makes good' story. Yet the local papers, in their full-page obituaries, did not mention the little draper's shop in Chesham above which he was born. Sir Arthur, they recorded – as did the national press – was the eldest of three sons and five daughters of a Nottingham lace manufacturer. It was when Arthur was eight that his parents moved to Nottingham, where his Uncle George had a lace warehouse. While the family was settling down there, Arthur was sent to live with his aunt, Mrs Robert Vernon of High Wycombe, where he attended Miss Heath's school. Later, when his father was prospering, he was sent as a boarder to University School, Nottingham. Most of his holidays were spent at his mother's home, Chartridge Farm, and a letter written by one of his cousins there shows how deeply attached he was to the Chiltern countryside. At school, his favourite amusements were theatricals and scene painting, his best subjects English

9

Arthur and Rebecca Liberty, parents of the founder of Liberty & Co. Oil paintings in the possession of A. I. Stewart-Liberty

From the *Chesham Companion to the Almanacks for the Town & Neighbourhood for the years 1845, 1846, & 1847*. Published by W. Hepburn, Chesham

literature and history. He was considered exceptionally intelligent and was entered rather young for a university scholarship, which he failed to get. He could not try again the following year as his father was in financial low water and could not keep him at school. Temporarily he was given a place in his uncle's lace warehouse, and then sent to be a clerk in the warehouse of another uncle who owned a wine business in London. He was still only sixteen.

It was hoped that this uncle might find some promising opening in the City for his intelligent young nephew. But a letter from Arthur to his mother on May 6, 1859, tells her that his uncle's business had become 'really dreadful and it makes him so miserable and without any spirit that I don't think he can take any interest or use his influence in getting me into any situation. Do you think I should be able to do better if I returned to Nottingham?' We do not know what his mother replied. What we do know is that soon after writing that letter Arthur was apprenticed to Mr John Weekes, a draper in Baker Street. It must have been the very opening that Arthur, with his artistic leanings, his interest in the theatre and painting, most earnestly did not want.

He found both the shop and the customers – and Mr Weekes himself – frustratingly old-fashioned. Mr Weekes for his part found his reluctant apprentice unpromising material. The apprenticeship was cut short after two years by mutual consent. But at least Arthur had moved from the City to the West End, and such free time as his long working hours allowed could be spent in visiting art galleries and public libraries, saving up such money as he could for the occasional visit to a theatre gallery. He must often have walked up and down Regent Street, the most famous shopping street in the world, designed by one of Britain's most famous architects, John Nash – the first London street ever to have been planned and built as a shopping street. In Regent Street it was strictly enforced that no butchers, public houses, greengrocers or other domestic trades were permitted, and no hawkers or street vendors allowed. It was for the luxury trades. Indeed it was described by Augustus Sala in 1858 as 'an avenue of superfluities, a great trunk-road in Vanity Fair'. And from its completion in 1820 it had been a fashionable rendezvous, where horse-riders and carriages, the equipages of 'the nobility and gentry' jostled with each other every afternoon during the season. 'Only here,' wrote Francis Wey, a visiting Frenchman, 'Only here could you find the fashionable world so perfectly at home in the middle of the street.' [1]

Clearly, if one were condemned to work in the drapery trade, one could

[1] *A Frenchman Sees the English in the 'Fifties.* Adapted from the French of Francis Wey by Valerie Pirie. Sidgwick and Jackson, 1935.

not aim higher than Regent Street where half the shops had Royal Warrants. And Arthur Liberty succeeded in getting a post at the highly esteemed establishment of Farmer & Rogers' Great Shawl and Cloak Emporium that occupied Nos 171, 173, and 175 on the west side of Regent Street. Farmer & Rogers had taken over J. and J. Holmes's Shawl Emporium, shawl manufacturers by appointment to H.M. the Queen, to H.M. the Duchess of Kent, and several other H.M.s. The shawl business was at its height by the late 1850s, the fashion having grown in importance from 1830 onwards, when skirts began increasing in volume. The more voluminous skirts became, the more difficult it was to wear fitted mantles or jackets with them. By the time the crinoline proper arrived (it held sway for about ten years from 1856), shawls were worn outdoors as well as indoors. A little book called *A Visit to Regent Street*, published by the printer and engraver Henry Vizetelly about two years before Arthur Liberty's arrival at Farmer & Rogers', described the Great Shawl and Cloak Emporium: 'This renowned emporium is the most celebrated of its kind in Europe. It has this season been thoroughly re-decorated in most superb style, besides undergoing considerable alteration to meet the exigencies of increased trade, and afford additional comfort to the numerous visitors. India, China, French, Paisley, Norwich, and Fancy Shawls – every description of cloak and jacket for the carriage, promenade, and opera.'

The year that Arthur Liberty joined Farmer & Rogers was the year of the International Exhibition of 1862. It was held in Kensington, on the site later used for the Natural History Museum, and was the event of the year. Walter Crane, then a young man, wrote of it later in *An Artist's Reminiscences*:

'There was a fine, representative group of the Pre-Raphaelite Brotherhood's pictures, including some of Madox Brown's finest works. English decorative art, too, began to assert itself in this exhibition. There was a most interesting group of furniture and examples of interior decoration of all kinds shown by the Ecclesiological Society, among which, I think, there was early work of J. Sedding, the architect, Pugin, William Burges, Philip Webb, William Morris, and E. Burne-Jones. One saw in the work of these men the influence of the Gothic revival and the study of mediaeval art generally. Their painted furniture and rich embroideries had previously only been seen by close friends.'

It was, in fact, the first time that the work of Morris, Marshall & Faulkner Company (founded the previous year) had been publicly exhibited; and the display included a sofa by Rossetti, sideboards and washstand by Philip Webb, tiles by Rossetti, Burne Jones, Webb and Morris; also a substantial range of joiner-made 'mediaeval' furniture.

The part of the Exhibition that most excited Arthur Liberty was the Japanese section. It was the first time Japan had shown at a European exhibition, and the section included the personal collection of the first British Minister in Japan, Sir Rutherford Alcock: lacquer, bronzes, porcelain, everything exquisitely different from the products of Victorian England. When the exhibition closed, some of the Japanese exhibits were bought by Farmer & Rogers and formed the basis for an Oriental Warehouse that they opened next door to their main

Arthur Lasenby Liberty aged 21 years, 1864

shop. Liberty was the junior of two young men chosen to work in the Oriental Warehouse; and two years later he was promoted to become its manager.

Trade winds from Japan had been stirring a little before the International Exhibition of 1862. Two and a half centuries previously, in 1624, Japan had forbidden access to her ports except to the Dutch, limiting her own building of ships to small vessels so that Japanese seamen could not navigate in the open sea and come into contact with other nations. Thus theirs became an isolated culture, uninfluenced by the rest of the world. But after the revolution of 1848, a few contacts with Western nations began besides those with the Dutch. Then in 1853 Commodore Perry sailed a squadron of the United States fleet into the Bay of Yedo, and during the following years there was intermittent contact through American and British navy personnel. In 1854 an exhibition of Japanese applied art was held in the gallery of the Old Water Colour Society in Pall Mall East, from which the Science and Art Department (the origin of the Victoria & Albert Museum) made purchases on the recommendation of Henry Cole. But there was little press comment at the time, and it seems to have been very much a connoisseur's occasion. Then in 1858 Japan signed a limited commercial treaty with Britain and America.

In Paris, two years before that treaty, the painter and etcher Felix Bracquemond discovered a paper-covered book of wood-block prints by Hokusai used as packing for some imported oriental china. It was these prints that excited James McNeill Whistler who was then living in Paris, and influenced his work so greatly. Other prints came to light in the same way; and only two years later, in 1858, a series of roller-printed cottons with designs originating directly from Japanese prints was produced by Daniel Lee of Manchester. In Paris, a shop for the sale of oriental *objets d'art* was established the same year. It was in the rue de Rivoli, run by Madame de Soye, who named her shop *La Porte Chinoise*. Baudelaire, the brothers de Goncourt, Manet, Fantin-Latour, and Whistler were among those who made it a meeting ground. The talk was of *l'art pour l'art*, which became translated in England into 'art for art's sake'. Art for art's sake meant art that did not tell a story. It meant art with no moral to preach, no religious faith to inspire, no social message, no commitment, no reason to exist except to be beautiful.

In London, after Farmer & Rogers had opened their Oriental Warehouse, the apostles of art for art's sake tended to use it as a meeting place in the same way as their contemporaries in Paris were using *La Porte Chinoise*. Here they came in search of blue-and-white porcelain and other oriental enchantments. They acquired ginger jars decorated with prunus and blackthorn blossom, and the tall vases which Whistler, now moved to London, called 'Long Elizas' from their Dutch name 'Lange Lysen'. Arthur Liberty served the artists and, so to speak, absorbed them – their talk, their enthusiasms, their audacious pronouncements upon life and upon art. Some fifty years later he spoke of this time in an interview with the *Daily Chronicle*. He told how 'famous artists got the idea that I took a real interest in what we sold and my knowledge and appreciation of art were extended by prolonged visits to their studios, where I was always made welcome. The soft, delicate coloured fabrics of the East particularly attracted these artists because they could get nothing of European make that would drape properly [*on their artist's models*] and which was of sufficiently well-balanced colouring to satisfy the eye. Albert Moore found them so helpful that he gave me a beautiful drawing of a group of classical figures holding up some of these draperies'. In the same interview, Arthur Liberty told the reporter that Ellen Terry was one of his closest friends, and that on one occasion he took part with her in a rehearsal of a Tom Taylor play which, however, was never produced.

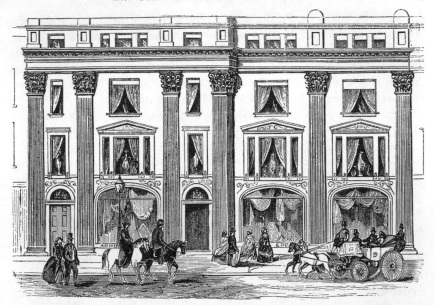

Farmer & Rogers' Great Shawl & Cloak Emporium, 171–5 Regent Street.
From *A Visit to Regent Street, c.* 1860

Ellen Terry's elder sister Kate, considered an even more brilliant actress than Ellen, married Arthur Lewis, partner in the prosperous firm of Lewis & Allenby, Silk Mercers to H.M. the Queen. Their shop was at 195 Regent Street, a little further north on the same side of the street as Farmer & Rogers', between New Burlington Street and Conduit Street: and in 1866 they built impressive new premises round the corner in Conduit Street, a five-storey building with all the dignified appearance of a Pall Mall club.

It may have been through Arthur Lewis that Arthur Liberty met the Terry family. Indeed, it may have been through Arthur Lewis, or the Terrys, that he met Martha Cottam, whom he married on June 8, 1865, at St Pancras Church. Nothing more is known of this first wife of Arthur Liberty, although it is believed in the family that she was an actress. Nor has it proved possible to trace when, or how, the marriage ended. Maybe it lasted no longer than the brief marriage of Ellen Terry to the painter G. F. Watts. Artistic circles converged with stage circles, especially at Little Holland House, where Mrs Prinseps was a dominating hostess and G. F. Watts a permanent fixture as her protégé. The grounds of Moray Lodge, the house that Arthur Lewis bought in 1862, bordered on those of Holland House; and when he was a bachelor he used to give extravagant Bohemian parties, his guests including the Pre-Raphaelite artists, George du Maurier and Leech, Thackeray and Trollope, Mr Poole the tailor and Mr Tattersall the horse-dealer. He had travelled a great deal on the Continent, was deeply interested in music, and was one of the founders of the Arts Club in 1863. The fact that his business was retail trade was a social disadvantage that he had overcome, not just by his wealth but by his wide cultural interests.

How great a social disadvantage it was to be a retailer in mid-Victorian times is shown by an entry relating to Arthur Lewis in A. J. Munby's diary: [1] '*Thursday 2 June, 1859.* Went, about 12, with Severn to a Bachelor's Ball at St. James's Hall: to which we were invited, at Vaux's party, by a pleasant gentlemanly man named Lewis, the son and partner of the *mercer* in Regent Street! [*Munby's italics and exclamation mark*] – Lewis being modest and accomplished and having the wisdom not to be ashamed of his position, is much liked in good male society.' Munby himself, an unsuccessful barrister, very minor poet, and occasional contributor to literary reviews, wrote of the rich tradesmen's families at the ball: 'Their equality in wealth, dress, and circumstances only makes the true inferiority more evident. The men were better than the women: but this was only because a good many gentlemen, properly so called, were present.'

Munby's diary entry was before Arthur Lewis acquired Moray Lodge, with its stables and large garden, and began his famous hospitality – before, also, he founded the Arts Club, whose membership included Charles Dickens, Walter Severn, Lord Houghton, James Whistler – and A. J. Munby.

After Arthur Lewis's marriage to Kate Terry, the parties at Moray Lodge became less Bohemian, taking the form of musical evenings to which came 'all that was most select in the circle of the fine arts, the stage, literature, and music, with a sprinkling of High Society'.[2] Their eldest daughter, Kate Terry Lewis, wrote in her autobiography that Arthur Lewis's announcement of his engagement to an actress came as a terrible shock to his family. His mother, to whom the stage was perdition, was only reconciled when Kate consented to retire altogether from the stage – she was only twenty-three, and already London's leading actress. 'Arthur must have been bewitched,' lamented Mrs Lewis. Whether Arthur Liberty was also bewitched by an actress has proved impossible to establish. What is certain is that he was in no position, as was Arthur Lewis, to capture a leading actress and command her retirement from the stage. Perhaps Martha Cottam was an artists' model; but

[1] *Munby, Man of Two Worlds, The Life and Diary of Arthur J. Munby, 1828–1910* by Derek Hudson. John Murray, 1972.
[2] *A Victorian Painter – Luke Fildes*, RA. By L. V. Fildes. Michael Joseph, 1968.

again she would not have been a famous one like Whistler's Jo, or Rossetti's Annie Miller. At the time of the marriage he was only a twenty-two year old shop manager, with no income except his weekly wage.

When he was thirty, and had been manager of the Oriental Warehouse for ten years, he felt justified in expecting some advancement in the firm. He had built up the Oriental side of Farmer & Rogers' until it had become the most profitable part of the firm. He asked to be taken into partnership, but they refused, saying that the business would not stand another partner. His artist friends urged him to start a shop of his own, promising to transfer their custom to him from Farmer & Rogers. He himself confidently believed that, if only he had a free hand, he could change the whole look of fashion – in clothes, as well as interior decoration. He saw fashion taking the soft, languid, flowing look of the draperies worn in Pre-Raphaelite paintings, a look that other women could achieve by dressing with his fabrics. And by 1874 he had an added incentive for his ambition to found his own business: he had become engaged to Emma Louise Blackmore.

226   FUN.   [MAY 30, 1874.

A WALK DOWN REGENT STREET.

2

THE FIRST HALF-SHOP
JAPANESE BONANZA

Emma Louise Blackmore was two years younger than Arthur. The Black-
mores were a Devonshire family from Littleham near Exmouth, but Emma
Louise's father, Henry Blackmore, had moved to London and established a
West End tailoring business in Brook Street. Some notes written by his
grandson Harold Blackmore tell how Emma Louise persuaded her father –
coerced him, when it came to the crunch – into putting up the money for
Arthur to start his own shop . . . 'Two men more opposite in their general
ideas than my grandfather and Arthur Liberty would have been difficult to
find, as my grandfather was a very correct early Victorian.' The notes
continue:

'My aunt [*that is Emma Louise*] told me that when the half-shop in Regent
Street in which the business started had been taken on lease, it had been on
the understanding that my grandfather would put up £1,500 and back a Bill
for Arthur Liberty with Henry Hill, the tailor in Bond Street, for another
thousand pounds. By that time my grandfather had become to some extent
mental and was under the impression he had no money at all, and he absolutely refused to sign a cheque which he said could not be met, or to back a
Bill which he felt he had no possibility of meeting. This put them in a pretty
bad hole, and eventually my aunt had to stand over him and make him sign.
The £1,500 was paid off out of the first year's profits and I think the Bill also,
or at any rate very shortly afterwards.
    'The marriage was at All Souls, South Hampstead, on September 25th,
1875, and the wedding breakfast was at my grandfather's house, No. 7
Fairfax Road, Hampstead. I was only four years old, but I remember it
because my aunt wanted me to kiss her, but I had some sort of feeling that
Arthur Liberty wouldn't like it, and so I refused. They went to Paris for
their honeymoon, where Arthur picked up a pair of Chinese vases, which
more than paid the whole expenses of the honeymoon. When they returned

they lived with my grandfather in Fairfax Road. My aunt went into the cash desk the first Christmas.'

Arthur Liberty in later life often paid tribute to the aid he had from his father-in-law, and to his wife's help in starting the first shop. He added on one occasion: 'Frugality also aided success, for many years all profits were left in the business. This of course is an act of self-denial that is not always possible.' It was possible for the young Libertys because they were living rent free in Henry Blackmore's house. During this time Arthur evidently proved to his father-in-law that he was not just an irresponsible Bohemian, in spite of the 'artistic' dress he affected: velvet jacket, low turned-over collar, informal necktie. For when Henry Blackmore died in 1881 he left the house in Fairfax Road to Arthur Liberty and his tailoring business to his daughter. Emma Louise ran it for some years with a manager, and used to go in once a week to sign cheques and look over the returns. Young Harold, who often stayed with them at Fairfax Road and later at 13 Cornwall Terrace, Regent's Park, remembered going in with his aunt to the business at Brook Street, and then on the very short distance to Uncle Arthur's shop . . . 'One of my earliest recollections in connection with the Liberty shop was the Electrical Exhibition which was held in the Crystal Palace about 1878. Liberty's had a furnished cottage erected in the Palace, wired for electric light. The entrance fee charged was 6d per head, and you entered the cottage in perfect darkness; the assistant then turned on the switch, and everybody said "Oh!".'

It was only half a shop that Arthur Liberty acquired – No. 218A Regent Street – but he grandly named it East India House. On the day of the opening on May 15, 1875, he had three employees: William Judd from Farmer & Rogers', Hannah Browning who was a girl of sixteen, and Hara Kitsui a Japanese boy. He had only intended to have the girl and the boy, thinking he could not afford a man. But what happened he told in a speech many years later: 'On the morning my business was started, I had arranged for a staff of two assistants when lo! to my surprise three instead of two were busy at work, and I found that the third was a volunteer who declared he had resolved to follow my fortunes "Yea or nay, pay or no pay".'

William Judd also spoke of that first morning to reporters when, fifty years later, he was invited to open the new Tudor building: 'I remember when there were only four of us – the Master, two others, and myself. Now there's a thousand or more. We just sold coloured silks from the East – nothing else. The sort of thing that William Morris, Alma Tadema and Burne-Jones and Rossetti used to come in and turn over and rave about.'

Emma Louise Blackmore and Arthur Lasenby Liberty at the time of their betrothal, 1874

Hannah Browning, long after she had retired, wrote her recollections of the early days for the staff magazine, the *Liberty Lamp*:

'I was a girl of 16½ years when I found myself one day in May, 1875, installed as one of three with Mr Judd. Yes! a sort of "make yourself useful" person, being cashier, saleswoman, duster, etc.; and I assure the firm as it is today, that the interests of that business of Mr A. L. Liberty were mine; a good business day for him meant joy to me and the reverse meant disappointment. I was the only female for some time, but Mr Judd will bear me out in saying that he and I were always good pals. After being disappointed in several clerks, Mr Liberty decided to teach me to take on that post, and as I look back and smile at my stupid mistakes, I realise the patience of he who undertook the task.'

The little shop was not long restricted to fabrics only, and very soon the second half of the premises was taken over. The *Liberty Lamp* has some more recollections by William Judd:

'Our time was 8 o'clock in the morning till finished, and we closed at 7.30. When the other half of the shop was taken over, Mr Liberty had part of the adjoining wall broken through, making two arches into the next half shop; but as a proper settlement had not been made, the arch had to be replaced, which was done that night and made as it was before. One of Mr Liberty's early purchases was a lot of Japanese gods, Buddhas, etc. of all sizes. The four largest were very old and in too bad condition to sell, so Hara Kitsui and myself in our spare time took them to pieces and built them up again with tin tacks, putty and several coats of paint. They then occupied a conspicuous place on the balcony of East India House.

'In those days we were always changing the departments about. The carpets would be moved upstairs and the china down, etc. This was always done after closing time and all finished before we left, also a lot of structural work was done; staircases taken down and opened up somewhere else and rooms and doorways altered. About then we got into touch with many well-known artists, and anything that was especially good and rare in embroidery or lacquer or cloisonné enamel, or Satsuma ware, I often had to take for them to see.'

The artists who had foregathered at Farmer & Rogers' Oriental Warehouse were now meeting on the opposite side of Regent Street, at Arthur Liberty's little shop. And Farmer & Rogers' closed down soon after Liberty left: it transpired that the Oriental Warehouse had been carrying the whole business, shawls having gone out of fashion with the crinoline. The influential architect and designer Edward W. Godwin, an early enthusiast for Japanese art and design, wrote a long article in *The Architect* of December 23, 1876, describing Liberty's shop and its customers. He said he had heard that a new importation of Japanese fans was about to be unpacked at 'the little shop near the top of Regent Street', so went along to be there at the opening of the cases:

'There was quite a crowd when we arrived. A distinguished traveller had buttonholed the obliging proprietor in one corner; a well-known baronet, waiting to do the same, was trifling with some feather dusting brushes; two architects of well-known names were posing an attendant in another corner with awkward questions; three distinguished painters with their wives blocked up the staircase; whilst a bevy of ladies filled up the rest of the floor space. Before I could catch the eye of the master of this enchanting cave, it was learned that the cases would not arrive till late in the evening. Almost in a moment the swarm of folk vanished, and I was free to pick my way from ground-floor to attics, for No. 218 Regent Street is from front to back and top to bottom literally crammed with objects of oriental manufacture.

'If it only had a little decent furniture, an artist might almost decorate and furnish his rooms from this one shop. There are matting and mats, carpets and rugs for the floor; Japanese papers for the walls; curtain stuffs for windows and doors; folding screens, chairs, stools, and so forth. There are necessarily some few things the banishment of which one could easily forgive. Most of the faience flower-pots, garden seats, vases, etc. are not only "rough" as the catalogue describes them, but positively crude, both in shape and colour. Now and then, too, one stumbles against a curtain or rug that is irritating in its sheer violence of colour. Such coarseness, however, is rarely or ever to be found even in the *modern* products of Japan. I say "rarely", but I confess, with not a little sadness and misgiving, that the rareness is lessening every day. Either the European market is ruining Japanese art, or the Japanese have taken our artistic measure and found it wanting; perhaps there is a little of both. Take for example the common paper fan of today and compare it with some imported here ten or even eight years ago. Those are for the most part lovely in delicate colour and exquisite in drawing, but most of today's fans are impregnated with the crudeness of the European's sense of colour, and are immeasurably beneath the older examples.'

One wonders what Godwin's assessment would have been of the Japanese sunshades at one shilling each which William Judd sold for Liberty's on a Bank Holiday during an exhibition at Alexandra Palace, where they had fitted out a Japanese house . . . 'Two cases were quickly sold out,' Mr Judd reported.

Godwin's criticism in *The Architect* continued:

'There is one inexpensive article, however, the little lacquer ash tray selling for sixpence, that bears the unmistakable impress of that artistic nation to which so many of us are directly or indirectly indebted. On one are a bit of old weather-beaten bamboo and a butterfly; on another, one plant of the iris, with two blossoms and three buds; on a third, a few naked branches; on a fourth, a baby bamboo shooting up like an arrow, each and all designed with a felicity and drawn with a freedom, and withal a delicacy, that is unmatchable by any other nation.

'To an architect one of the most interesting modern imports is the leather-like embossed paper made in pieces twelve yards long and one yard wide. There is one – a broad pattern of dark green meandering foliage on a gold ground – which is extremely beautiful and, properly placed, might be well used in almost any style of building, and would of itself give a style to a house that had none. There are others that are more singular than beautiful, and seem far better adapted for filling up the small panels of cheap furniture than for any extensive area on walls.'

Godwin had been one of the first in England to start collecting Japanese prints, when he was a young architect living in Bristol in the early 1860s. He wrote the theatre criticisms in the local paper, and his articles were as much comments on décor and costume as on acting and production. When in 1863 Ellen Terry appeared as Titania at the re-opening of the Theatre Royal, Bath, he designed her dress. 'We made it at his house in Bristol,' she wrote in her memoirs.[1] 'He showed me how to damp it and "wring" it while it was wet, tying up the material as the Orientals do in their "tie and dry" process, so that when it was dry and untied, it was all crinkled and clinging. This was the first lovely dress I ever wore.' She was sixteen at the time, and it was four years later, after her separation from G. F. Watts, that she began living with Godwin in Hertfordshire. In 1874, when they moved to Taviton Street, Bloomsbury, even their children's nursery walls were covered with Japanese prints. Whistler gave Ellen a blue-and-white Nankin dinner set, and 'sent my little girl a tiny Japanese kimono when Liberty was hardly a name'. The drawing-room has been described by the actor Johnstone Forbes-Robertson, who visited them when he was an art student:

'The floor was covered with straw-coloured matting, and there was a dado of the same material. Above the dado were white walls, and the hangings were of cretonne, with a fine Japanese pattern in delicate grey-blue. The chairs were of wickerwork, cushions like the hangings, and in the centre of the room was a full-sized cast of the Venus of Milo, before which was a small pedestal holding a censer from which rose, curling round the Venus, ribbons of blue smoke. The whole effect was what art students of my time would have called "awfully jolly".'

The Taviton Street ménage came to an end the year before Godwin's account of Liberty's shop in which he expressed distress at the deterioration to be detected in many Japanese imports. There had been no trade restrictions with Japan since the Royal Revolution of 1868, and Japanese goods were pouring into England, Japanese warehouses springing up in London, Oriental Departments opening in some of the more enterprising of the growing department stores – William Whiteley's, Debenham & Freebody, Swan & Edgar. The demand could not be filled by the irregular output of individual craftsmen and artists, so it was being met with hastily produced

[1] *The Story of My Life* by Ellen Terry. Hutchinson, 1908.

Nankin vase with Kylin top 'boldly decorated in blue-and-white with landscape and figure subjects; 36 inches high, 15 gns per pair. Recommended for vestibules, staircases, etc.' Porcelain catalogue, c. 1885

The top part of this advertisement is similar to the Liberty & Co. bill heading c. 1880

trash. The distinguished Dr Christopher Dresser (a friend of Arthur Liberty, whose son Louis joined the furnishing department in 1896) had himself visited Japan immediately after the Revolution, having been commissioned by the British Chamber of Commerce to report on Japanese manufactures. Thus he saw the creative work of the country before their production became westernised. In 1879 he started a short-lived Japanese Warehouse in Farringdon Street, then in 1880 a shop in New Bond Street called Dresser's Art Furniture Alliance, in which the 'attendants' were robed in aesthetic costume of 'demure art colours'. The swift demise of the Japanese Warehouse was probably caused by the difficulty of maintaining the high standard of imports demanded by his discriminating taste. His Art Furniture Alliance sold metalwork, furniture, glass and pottery, mostly designed by Dresser himself.

Arthur Liberty did not have Christopher Dresser's first-hand knowledge of Japan, but his taste had been formed by the early imports he had handled at Farmer & Rogers'. He realised that the Japanese bonanza was getting out of hand, and began to seek other sources of oriental merchandise . . . India,

China, Java, Indo-China, Persia. He still considered Eastern fabrics to be his most important speciality, but was finding it impossible to obtain sufficient supplies to satisfy the demand that he himself had created. Furthermore, it had become apparent that many of the Eastern fabrics were too delicate, or their dyes too fugitive, for the use to which they were being put by dressmakers and interior decorators. Another worry was that the Eastern producers were beginning to change their subtle tints for the cruder colours they believed the Western hemisphere preferred. So he set about persuading English firms to experiment with Eastern dyeing techniques, English textile manufacturers to adapt their machines to weaving processes that would produce fabrics similar to those of the East. Like William Morris, he wanted to improve the nation's taste by giving ordinary people the chance to buy beautiful things. But unlike Morris, he believed that machines could be brought to the service of art, and that this was essential since handmade things would always be too expensive for any but the well-off – as, indeed, most of Morris's productions proved to be.

At first Liberty concentrated upon importing plain woven piece goods, undyed: the soft woollens of Cashmere, the filmy gauzes of India, the fine light cottons familiar in tropical countries, the silks of China and Japan – mostly plain-woven, but some with a small damask pattern. They included the tussore or 'wild silk' produced by the worm fed on the oak, as well as the true 'bombyx' fed on the mulberry. Tussore silk in its natural colour had been fashionable for many years as fabric for dresses and light furnishings, but no means had been found for bleaching and dyeing it, and its use had also been handicapped by its narrow width. Now Liberty representatives in India persuaded the weavers to use a wider loom, and new processes for dyeing it were evolved in England.

Liberty's greatest triumph in those early days came from a co-operation with Thomas Wardle, the dyers and printers of Leek in Staffordshire, who also worked for William Morris. Between them, Liberty and Wardle introduced dyes which had until then been supposed to be a closely guarded secret of the East . . . delicate pastel tints which they called 'Art Colours', and that became described all over the world as 'Liberty colours'. Silks in Liberty colours were an influential element in the Aesthetic Movement. Liberty's windows had white painted fretwork screens, and the silks were draped in front of these in graduated tints. They became one of the sights of Regent Street . . . a revelation to a generation accustomed to the harsh colours of aniline dyes, to stiff silks, bombasine and alpaca. The Liberty silks were soft and pliant, without 'finish' or 'dressing', or any of the processes used by manufacturers to give 'body' or a meretricious silky surface to cheap fabrics. The irregularity of the hand weaving, which gave them an accidental play of light, was another of their charms. It was not only artists and aesthetes who were enraptured by them. *Sylvia's Home Journal*, essentially a bourgeois publication, wrote of them in 1879: 'The texture of them is so pure and fine that they adapt themselves particularly to the present style of dress . . . Indian silks in reds so soft that not even the most rubicond wearer could vulgarize them; greens and blues so indefinite that it is difficult to class them *as* greens and blues. They wash like a silk handkerchief.'

A member of the Liberty staff, looking back from the 1920s, recalled how they were used for decoration: 'Our Founder imported large quantities of Indian, Chinese, and Japanese silks to be dyed. They "caught on" with the public and literally *miles* of them were sold for draping purposes, often caught up and otherwise mingled with fans and hand-screens. In summer, the heavy poles and curtains were taken down and windows draped with the silks in different shades of the same colour, hung in festoons. Sometimes the large chimney glasses were lowered to the floor, and when draped with the silks the result was a not unpleasing illusion of the entrance to another room. People found that an ugly Victorian room, with its gilt chimney glasses, walnut furniture of bastard French design, repp curtains and crochet antimacassars, which could boast nothing but an intense respectability, could be made comparatively interesting and brightened at a very small outlay, and East India House was besieged.'

Japanese god on the balcony of
East India House

3

THE AESTHETIC MOVEMENT; WHISTLER
OSCAR WILDE, 'PATIENCE'

With all this furore for his fabrics, Arthur Liberty was able to acquire the second half of the shop at 218 Regent Street within eighteen months, as well as repay his father-in-law's loan. The aesthetic climate nourished his artistic leanings, and he began to blossom as a virtual impresario of the decorative arts.

It was a time when interest in domestic design and decoration was being stimulated as never before. Twenty-five years earlier, the Great Exhibition of 1851 had aroused the nation's pride in her industrial supremacy and affirmed her leadership in the new machine age; but discriminating people had seen in the opulence of the manufactures, the incontinence of the ornamentation, the pomposity of the products, the lack of discipline in design, an alarming threat. Britain would soon be engulfed by a tide of vulgarity. Fortunately there were influences at work to counteract the tide, if not entirely to turn it. The lectures and writings of Ruskin, whose *Seven Lamps of Architecture* was published in 1849; the paintings and ideals of the Pre-Raphaelite Brotherhood founded by Rossetti and Holman Hunt the previous year; the foundation of William Morris's company of 'Fine Art Workmen' in 1861; the interest in Japanese art and crafts aroused by the Exhibition of 1862; the publication in 1868 of Charles Eastlake's *Hints on Household Taste*, advocating 'the simplest style, in an age of debased design', which went rapidly into four editions in England, six in America . . . all these things combined to make the decorative arts a topic of conversation beyond the immediate circles of professional artists, architects, and designers.

By the mid-1870s, the wits of the day divided Society into two camps: the aesthetes and the philistines. The main target of the wits was not the creative aesthete, but the contemplative aesthete who created nothing more permanent than conversation, who described art as life seen through a temperament, and made the simplest reaction to anything of beauty very very complicated. The *nouveaux riches* thrown up by the Industrial Revolution, although considered brash with their brass, had to be tolerated by practising artists since they were the new patrons of the arts. Francis R. Leyland of Liverpool, a self-made ship-owner, set out to be a modern Medici. He bought a house at 49 Prince's Gate, Knightsbridge, and had the interior rebuilt under the direction of Norman Shaw. Shaw was one of the most fashionable architects of the day, and was engaged the following year to complete Bedford Park, the original garden suburb planned as a Utopia fit for aesthetes to live in, the first eighteen houses of which had been designed by E. W. Godwin.

The rooms of Leyland's house were hung with paintings by Rossetti, Millais, Burne-Jones, Ford Madox Brown, Watts, Legros. Whistler's 'Princesse du Pays de la Porcelaine' was the sole picture in the diningroom, and Whistler protested that its effect was ruined by the walls being covered with Spanish leather painted with red flowers, the work of the designer Thomas Jeckyll. So Leyland, still in Liverpool, gave Whistler a free hand to redecorate the diningroom, and the artist held open house there to all his friends while working on his design of peacocks. The story of the subsequent quarrel over the fee of two thousand guineas is well known. Arthur Liberty in an interview years later said, 'Whistler always pretended that he valued my critical judgement, and certainly we had a feeling of sympathy on the Japanese impressionist side of things. I remember spending many hours with him when he was engaged on the famous peacock room, and it was a pleasant pose of his to suggest that I assisted him with advice. But no man, I suppose, was ever more independent of advice or less patient with it.' One of the things that Leyland most resented was that Whistler invited journalists to a Press view and gave them printed publicity leaflets about his design. According to two of Whistler's American biographers, these leaflets were also distributed in Liberty's shop, with a general invitation for anyone to come and see the work in progress.

The following year brought the even better known Whistler sensation – his libel action against John Ruskin. Ruskin had published a vitriolic criticism in his magazine *Fors Clavigera* of Whistler's nocturnes exhibited at the opening of the Grosvenor Gallery in Bond Street, writing of 'the ill-educated conceit of the artist that so nearly approaches the aspect of wilful imposture . . . asking two hundred guineas for flinging a pot of paint in the public's face'. Ruskin had long been regarded as an infallible authority upon matters of art, and his criticism could drastically affect the sales of Whistler's paintings. The trial that followed was in effect the trial of 'art for art's sake'. Whistler won the case, but it was only a moral victory – he was awarded only a farthing damages, and no costs. Arthur Liberty wrote to him a letter of congratulation and sympathy, to which Whistler replied: 'Of course "costs" would have been more satisfactory to the minds of some – but to the world really it has been a great moral victory – and the first shot at the critic has at last been fired. You know I always win in the end.' In the meantime, the costs made him bankrupt. The White House that Godwin had just finished building for him in Tite Street, Chelsea, had to be sold with all its contents – furniture, pictures, beloved blue-and-white china. Before he left it, Whistler climbed a ladder and wrote over the doorway: 'Except the Lord build the house, their labour is but lost that build it. E. W. Godwin, F.S.A. built this one'.

In 1878, Oscar Wilde came down from Oxford with First Class Honours and the Newdigate prize for poetry. He welcomed himself rapturously into the artistic and literary coteries of London, and soon became the most conspicuous apostle of the Aesthetic Movement. His poetic clothes had already been imitated by undergraduates and students of art colleges, who cultivated long hair, affected a way of speaking they imagined to be Wilde's, and extolled the writings of Walter Pater. George du Maurier had begun his brilliant mockery of the aesthetes in *Punch* the year before, and Oscar Wilde came as a gift from the gods. Oscar was the living embodiment of all the aspirations of Postlethwaite and Maudle, the consummate ideal of the Cimabue Browns of Passionate Brompton, the 'lion' that Mrs Ponsonby de Tomkyns, pursuing the latest craze for what *Punch* called 'cultchah', would most wish to secure for her drawingroom evenings. Du Maurier worked the aesthetic vein until 1881, in May of which year *Punch* had a poem on the Grosvenor Gallery . . .

> The haunt of the very aesthetic,
> Here come the supremely intense,
> The long-haired and hyper-poetic,
> Whose sound is mistaken for sense.
> And many a maiden will mutter,
> When Oscar looms large on her sight,
> 'He's quite too consummately utter,
> As well as too utterly quite.'

That same year F. C. Burnand, then editor of *Punch*, wrote a comedy named *The Colonel* – in which the character of Lambert Stryke, played by Beerbohm Tree, satirised Wilde. It was the play in which the principal lady breathes the immortal words: 'There is so much to be learned from a teapot.' While *The Colonel* was still running, Gilbert and Sullivan's *Patience, or Bunthorne's*

THE SIX-MARK TEA-POT.

Æsthetic Bridegroom. "It is quite consummate, is it not?"
Intense Bride. "It is, indeed! Oh, Algernon, let us live up to it!"

By George du Maurier. *Punch*,
October 30, 1880

"O. W."

"O, I feel just as happy as a bright Sunflower!"
Lays of Christy Minstrelsy.

'Punch's Fancy Portraits No.
37'. *Punch*, June 25, 1881

Bride was produced at the Opéra Comique in London, first performance April 23, 1881. Durward Lely played Bunthorne, the fleshly poet in rivalry with the idyllic poet Archibald Grosvenor for the love of the village milkmaid, Patience. Some years previously Swinburne and Rossetti had been attacked in a pamphlet named *The Fleshly School*, but Durward Lely's appearance was that of Whistler, complete with his monocle. Archibald Grosvenor was unmistakably Oscar Wilde . . .

> Though the Philistine may jostle, you will rank as an apostle in the high aesthetic band,
> If you walk down Piccadilly with a poppy or a lily in your mediaeval hand.

Wilde had done just that, attired in a loose shirt with Byron collar and large knotted green tie, velvet knee-breeches, silk stockings and velvet beret. He was taking a madonna lily in homage to the fashionable beauty, Lillie Langtry.

In both *The Colonel* and *Patience*, Liberty fabrics were used for the costumes, many of those in *Patience* being designed by Gilbert himself. And Liberty 'artistic silks' were advertised in the programmes. When the opera was moved to D'Oyly Carte's newly-built Savoy Theatre, Liberty's design team decorated a little reception room there for the Prince of Wales, festooning it with silks. Similar work was also undertaken at Covent Garden Opera House, the Haymarket Theatre, Drury Lane, and the Lyceum. When D'Oyly Carte was preparing *The Mikado*, Liberty sent special envoys to Japan to study the clothes worn there and bring back exactly the right materials to costume the cast and dress the stage sets. He himself always had a box for the first nights of Gilbert and Sullivan operas.

In *Patience* the contrast between aesthetes and others was emphasised by the uniforms in bright primary colours of the army officers whose attentions were rebuffed by the chorus of soulful maidens. They would have found the officers infinitely more attractive if they had been dressed in 'a cobwebby grey velvet, with a tender bloom like cold gravy'. And colour again was the main theme in the lyric containing the verses:

> A Japanese young man,
> A blue and white young man,
> Francesca di Rimini, miminy pimimy,
> *Je-ne-sais-quoi* young man!

> A pallid and thin young man,
> A haggard and lank young man,
> A greenery-yallery, Grosvenor Gallery,
> Foot-in-the-grave young man!

Well known as these verses are, few who quote them now are likely to have more than a vague idea of what was meant by greenery-yallery. Here then is a description of Liberty's Umritza Cashmere, introduced by the firm in 1879, and described by a contemporary journalist in *Queen* magazine: 'There are tints that call to mind French and English mustards, sage-greens, willow-greens, greens that look like curry, and greens that are remarkable on lichen-coloured walls, and also among marshy vegetation – all of which will be warmly welcomed by those who indulge in artistic dress or in decorative revivals.'

Umritza Cashmere was one of Liberty's early fabric triumphs. He realised that, deliciously soft as were the native hand-woven cashmeres, they would not wear well. After many experiments with English weavers, he succeeded in producing a fabric that was greeted with songs of praise in all the fashion magazines. The English edition of *Le Follet* wrote, 'No material can

FELICITOUS QUOTATIONS.

Hostess (of Upper Tooting, showing new house to Friend). "WE'RE VERY PROUD OF THIS ROOM, MRS. HOMPSY. OUR OWN LITTLE UPHOLSTERER DID IT UP JUST AS YOU SEE IT, AND ALL OUR FRIENDS THINK IT WAS *LIBERTY!*"
Visitor (sotto voce). "'OH, LIBERTY, LIBERTY, HOW MANY CRIMES ARE COMMITTED IN THY NAME!'"

Punch, October 20, 1894

be calculated so thoroughly to display the qualities of softness, suppleness, lightness, warmth and graceful draping as the Oriental fabrics sold by Messrs Liberty. A recent introduction, Umritza Cashmere, possesses all the best qualities of the Indian make, combined with the durability and closeness of English manufactures. It is made in many neutral tints and all the art colours, and the long hairs scattered over its surface give it a very foreign appearance and add to its attractions.' This gratifying success led to other firms attempting imitations, but Liberty met these head on: 'As *imitation* is judged *the sincerest flattery*, Liberty & Co. draw attention, with considerable pride, to the many subsequent and present attempts by other firms to copy their UMRITZA CASHMERE.' None attempted to imitate the embroidered Umritza shawls which, about two yards square, sold from 84s. to 10 gns.

In January of the year after *Patience* was launched in London, Oscar Wilde started his American lecture tour. It lasted eighteen months, during which a New York production of *Patience* was running, and another company was on tour. One of Wilde's subjects was 'House Decoration', and the lectures were, indirectly, excellent publicity for Liberty's – as indeed was *Patience*. Everyone knew that Liberty of London was responsible for the original artistic fabrics of the aesthetes – 'art silk' and 'Liberty silk' had become synonymous terms. And everyone knew that Liberty's was the shop for aesthetic furnishings, for peacock's feathers and blue-and-white china, for Japanese fans and screens, for Japanese 'leather' wallpapers to make modish dadoes. Oscar Wilde's lecture tour may be said to have sown the first seeds that germinated into the long love affair between the Americans and Liberty's of London. Wilde repeated some of the lectures in England, and also lectured for the Rational Dress Society, of which his wife was an active member. Rational dress and aesthetic dress seem poles apart – what could be less aesthetic than Lady Harberton's dual garmenture? – but they had certain virtues in common, including the abandonment of corsets and the principle that all clothes should be loose and non-constrictive. Liberty's at this time did not make any actual clothes, but their fabrics were approved by dress reformers, and won a silver medal at the Rational Dress Exhibition at Kensington Town Hall in 1883. They were commended as playing 'an essentially prominent part in connection with Rational and Healthy dress'. Their healthiness came from their purity, their natural dyes, their unadulteration by any 'finish' or 'dressing', their freedom from any of the usual processes resorted to in order to impart a meretricious appearance of value to worthless materials. In his *Art and Decoration,* Oscar Wilde referred to a handbook written by E. W. Godwin for the organisers of the National Health Society Exhibition of 1884. In this Godwin had pointed out that some modification of Greek costume was perfectly applicable to the British climate if it was worn 'over a sub-stratum of pure wool, such as supplied by Dr Jaeger under the modern German system'. The principle was to suspend all apparel from the shoulders and 'rely for beauty not on the stiff, ready-made ornaments of the modern milliner, bows where there should be no bows, flounces where there should be no flounces, but on the exquisite play of light and line that one gets from rich and rippling folds'.

Liberty's LOTUS fabrics won a gold medal at the Amsterdam Exhibition of 1883, and their Art Fabrics Catalogue of that year describes some of the materials they were handling, while pointing out that almost daily they were receiving bales of silks which, on account of their great rarity and miscellaneous nature, it was impossible to catalogue. Nevertheless, those which

FTER many difficulties and a series of experiments, LIBERTY & Co. succeeded in inventing and bringing out the

⚜UMRITZA ✦ CASHMERE,⚜

which at once met with the most gratifying success, and has since steadily grown in favour. Below are a few criticisms from the leading dress journals, written at the time the material was first introduced, and great improvements have been made since, both in its finish and texture. Furthermore, as *imitation* is judged *the sincerest flattery*, LIBERTY & Co. draw attention, with considerable pride, to the many subsequent and present attempts by other firms, to copy their "UMRITZA CASHMERE."

Catalogue of 1883

were arriving sufficiently regularly to be included were of astonishing variety. There was Arabian cotton, 'a new and charming material for washing dresses, in ivory white and aesthetic colours'; Nagpur silk, hand-woven in India from the finest Bengal yarns, shipped in the raw state just as it comes from the looms, and dyed by a permanent process specially for Liberty & Co. There was Honan damask silk, and Mandarin brocaded silk 'in all the rare colours, for which the Chinese Mandarins' robes are famous'. There was Indian corah silk, tussore silk, shantung and pongee 'hand-woven from the Wild Silk of China, the cocoon of the Attacus Cynthia'. There were soft Rumchunder silks 'specially suitable for bridesmaids and evening dresses'; and white Shanghai silk 'very strong and soft, the best silk for underclothing'. This was sold in lengths of about 30 yards, 28" wide – clearly intended for making trousseaux of 'a dozen of each', as was mandatory for any Victorian bride.

The most expensive fabric in the catalogue was a 'Persian silk in woven designs, suitable for dressing gowns – *very rare*'. It was 10 guineas per piece of about six yards. But among those other imports too scarce to be catalogued, prices could also be much, much more rare. Ellen Terry in her *Story of My Life* relates that when in 1881 Henry Irving was producing Lord Tennyson's two-act tragedy *The Cup* at the Lyceum, with himself as Synorix and Ellen as Camma, they could not find precisely the right material for one of her dresses . . . 'But at last, poking about myself in quest of it, I came across the very thing at Liberty's, a saffron silk with a design woven into it by hand with many-coloured threads and little jewels. I brought a yard to rehearsal. It was declared perfect, but I declared the price prohibitive. "It's twelve guineas a yard, and I shall want yards and yards!" At the Lyceum, *wanton* extravagance was unknown.'

The upshot was that Arnott, the master carpenter, undertook to get something like it. This he did by dyeing twenty yards of raw silk the exact saffron, having two blocks made to print the design in red and black, and adding a few cheap spangles to replace the real jewels. Ellen Terry declared, 'On the stage, it looked better than the twelve guinea original.'

Catalogue of 1883

4

THE SHOP EXPANDS; HOWELL & JAMES
MERTON ABBEY

More space was urgently required, and when the lease of adjoining premises at 42 and 43 Kingly Street came on the market, Liberty acquired these. He also started a wholesale section at 7 Argyll Street, later moved to 2 Argyll Place. George Ensworth, who joined the staff in 1878, wrote some reminiscences in the *Liberty Lamp* nearly fifty years later:

'There were two shops, one on the south side being much smaller than the other, and a staff of thirteen all told, who were as follows: Messrs Carty (the manager, who lived with his wife and family on the premises); Goodyer; Haro Kerossake (Japanese); Timburg (apprentice); William Judd (packing and despatch, in charge); Alfred O'Brien (porter); Silvester Geary (porter) and Yours Truly; Misses Browning; Marley, Senr; Marley, Junr; Mary Judd (kitchen). The business at the commencement was entirely Oriental, "Importers from India, China and Japan" was the heading. Before entering 42 Kingly Street (the staff entrance) one had to ring a bell, and the door was opened by a pulley from the desk. At this desk, which was like an elongated cash desk, Mr Liberty worked with the two lady clerks, although a few months later he had an office to himself on the First Floor.'

There is very little to tell what Arthur Liberty was like as an employer in those early days, so one is grateful for George Ensworth's memory of him:

'I found him kind and considerate, perhaps a little irritable to some, but this would soon pass. Sometimes he would give me hints and advice for my benefit. On one occasion, while in his office, he said, "Do you smoke?" "No, sir." "If you take my advice you never will. I do, and you sometimes notice I am irritable. I think smoking is the cause." In cases of illness no-one could have been more kind and sympathetic. Once when I was away for a day with a bad cold, he wrote himself in reply to my letter, "You are not to return until your Aunt deems it prudent." His kind sympathy and respect shown to one very dear to me, will always remain deeply engraved in my memory.

'We closed at 7 o'clock and 4 o'clock on Saturdays; but a few years later Mr Liberty allowed half the Staff to leave at 2 o'clock on alternate Saturdays. Some years afterwards he decided to close the shop at 2 o'clock on Saturdays, and the Staff presented him with a piece of plate and an illuminated address at a Hall adjoining the Polytechnic. So it can well be said that our late respected Chief was a pioneer of the Early Closing Movement.

'My work was considerably more varied than that of the junior of today [*he is writing in 1925*]. I sometimes made a tour of the City Houses to match a piece of china, sometimes took "appro" goods to show, and the latter part of the day I would assist William Judd in addressing parcels and entering up the Parcels Book. We dined out in those days, with the exception of the lady-members of the Staff, who usually stated their requirements to Mary Judd; but tea was provided. It sometimes happened that Mary was away for a day and then her duties descended on me. On one occasion I got tea for Mr and Mrs Liberty and Mr Liberty's two sisters. I remember afterwards taking a plaque painted by Miss Octavia Liberty to Messrs Howell & James to be fired. The subject was, I think, Daffodils.'

Howell & James was a very distinguished establishment in Lower Regent Street, that at the beginning of the century had been Harding, Howell & Co., Grand Fashionable Magazine, of 89 Pall Mall. They sold silks, muslins, millinery, perfume, fans, and 'all articles of female dress and decoration in the first style of taste and fashion'. Rather surprisingly, they also sold wine. But the most important side of their business was that of furnishings, glass, and ceramics. It was Howell & James who in 1849 precipitated the collapse of the glittering but equivocal ménage of Lady Blessington and Count D'Orsay. This they did by putting in an execution for a debt of some thousands of pounds that Lady Blessington had incurred when furnishing Gore House. Geoffrey A. Godden in his *Victorian Porcelain* writes that from 1876 Howell & James held annual exhibitions of ceramic work by amateurs; and from George Ensworth's account of Octavia Liberty's 'Daffo-dils' plaque we learn that they undertook the firing of amateur work. 'Daffo-dils' may have been shown at one of their exhibitions which, Geoffrey Godden writes, 'were extremely popular and were patronised by Queen Victoria and other members of the Royal Family. A contemporary advertise-ment reads, "The Exhibition of 1878 contained upwards of one thousand original works – mostly by ladies – and was frequented during its two months' duration by nearly 10,000 visitors". Examples of amateurs' work can occasionally be found still bearing the original paper label of Howell & James, giving details of the painter, source of design, and date.' The Liberty family have no such trophy of Octavia's work, although they have a painting by her that won a gold medal at a Nottingham School of Art exhibition – a painting showing considerable talent and strong Pre-Raphaelite influence in colour and conception.

When Arthur bought his parents a new house in Mapperley Road, Nottingham, he had a studio constructed in it for Octavia. This sister was probably the one of his family most close to him in interests. His parents, though no doubt very proud of him, worried about his 'Bohemian' life in London: a letter from his father asks him to dress in a respectable manner when he was coming to a family dinner party, and not wear the 'extraordinary clothes' he sometimes appeared in. Octavia, as a young lady living at home, will have had little encouragement to wear aesthetic dress (which would have meant discarding her corsets), no chance at all to break out in a Bohemian phase. Indeed, her story has a truly Victorian ring about it. She became engaged to a widowed clergyman. Shortly before their marriage day he showed her round his house, and in the bridal chamber there hung a large photograph of his first wife over the bed. Octavia broke off the engagement abruptly, and remained a spinster.

Apart from the 'Daffodils' plaque, Howell & James has a place in the Liberty story because it was there that a brilliant young Welshman, John Llewellyn, worked before joining Liberty's in 1889 and rising to the Board within nine years. He brought with him from Howell & James the exclusive rights to sell Barum Ware, the pottery made by C. H. Brannam of Barnstaple. Another Liberty employee previously connected with Howell & James was A. W. Foster, who contributed his recollections to the *Liberty Lamp* of January, 1930:

'At the famous old business of Howell & James, silk mercers and wine merchants, who originally traded in a shop in Pall Mall, later used by the War Office, and still later by the Automobile Club, an old custom prevailed: coachmen and footmen, whose ladies were shopping inside, could by descending some steps under the shop window obtain beer and bread and cheese free. This was very popular. A specially prepared black grosgrain, made by Bonnet et Cie of Lyons, was supplied by this firm to Queen Victoria, 24 yards in each dress length, very ample proportions.

'Before becoming a servant of the great House of Liberty, when I represented Howell & James, on many occasions it was my privilege to take and show a selection of 16 yard lengths of Grosgrain in various shades (emphatically *not* Liberty!) to Mrs Dodds, the lady housekeeper at that time to the Princess of Wales at Marlborough House, to be distributed amongst the upper servants; of course, the final approval came from Her Royal Highness.' Evidently the servants required eight yards less for their dresses than Queen Victoria.

*　　*　　*　　*　　*

Once Arthur Liberty had established reliable supplies of imported silks and silks of oriental tints dyed in this country, he set about printing some of them with oriental designs. One of the first was Mysore Silk, woven by hand in India and shipped in the raw state just as it came from the looms. It was dyed in England 'by a permanent process especially for Liberty & Co.'; and then hand-printed by the wood block process. Most of the designs were exact reproductions of old Indian prints, 'obtained under exceptional

MYSORE ✠ SILK.

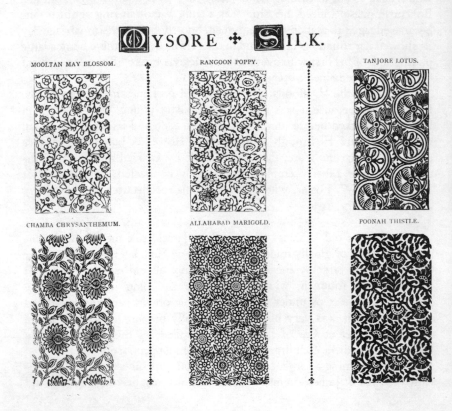

MOOLTAN MAY BLOSSOM.

RANGOON POPPY.

TANJORE LOTUS.

CHAMBA CHRYSANTHEMUM.

ALLAHABAD MARIGOLD.

POONAH THISTLE.

Hand-block printers on the bridge over the Wandle

The water wheel at Merton Abbey

facilities'. These exceptional facilities included consultation with authorities at the newly established Indian Museum. They were small floral designs, some printed in colours, some in gold, upon cream backgrounds, and were given evocative Eastern names. A collection of Liberty Silks printed by Thomas Wardle was shown at the Paris Exhibition of 1878, but soon most of the work was being done at Littler's block-printing works on the site of the pre-Reformation priory at Merton in Surrey.

Since the eighteenth century, a group of workshops built within the old priory walls beside the River Wandle had been used by a community of calico printers. The earliest is thought to have been William Halfhide, who is recorded as printing there in 1742. The meadows were intersected by ditches from which water was sprinkled over the calico to bleach it when spread on the grass. The River Wandle drove the mill wheels, one of which (restored and preserved by Liberty's) still exists – as does the flint and brick colour-house, which dates from 1743. About the beginning of the nineteenth century, Edmund Littler took over the buildings and the land to establish a block-printing business, which was continued by his son and grandson. The exact date when Littler first printed for Liberty is not known, but from the written recollections of members of Liberty & Co. it seems to have been within two years of the opening of the shop. By the nineties Liberty & Co. were taking up the whole of Littler's production.

It is generally assumed that Liberty went to Merton Abbey because William Morris had his printworks there. But Morris did not establish himself at Merton until 1881, so it would seem more likely that it was he who had heard through Liberty that Welch's calico printing works were for sale on the other side of the Wandle from Littler. Morris acquired a dwelling house, seven acres of meadows, and a group of tarred weatherboard and red tile buildings originally erected in the early eighteenth century by Huguenot refugees for use as a silk weaving factory. The Wandle supplied water of the special quality required for madder dyeing. Morris's property was down-stream from Littler's, which Liberty reckoned to their advantage . . . 'We sent our dirty water down to Morris.' Morris's associates at this time were Philip Webb the architect and furniture designer, Burne-Jones who supplied figure designs from his London studio, and William de Morgan, designer of lustre tiles and majolica, who had his own factory in Chelsea and supplied tiles to Liberty.

Until about 1900, there were partridges in the meadows, and John Llewellyn used to fish in the Wandle. It was considered one of the best trout streams in the south of England, which may well have been why there was a priory at Merton – the stew-ponds in which the monks stored their trout were still there when Liberty bought the printworks from Littler's in 1904. Most of the old buildings had become too dilapidated to repair, so had to be pulled down, but the last of the seven chapels of the Priory that had escaped destruction at the Reformation still remained. Henry VIII had many cart-loads of stone taken from Merton for the building of Nonsuch Palace. When Nonsuch in its turn was demolished, it is thought that some of the stone was used for the building of the old Epsom Grandstand, eight miles from Merton. Liberty's each year designed a Derby Day scarf, which was ready printed, wanting only the name of the winner. As soon as the race was over, a messenger was despatched on horse-back from the race course, and the winning horse's name was printed on the scarves. They were on sale in Merton High Street when the crowds came streaming back from Epsom.

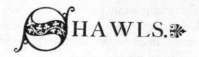

5

CHESHAM HOUSE; THE MOORISH CRAZE
ISADORA DUNCAN

About the year 1880 the ever growing shop in Regent Street, an exotic confusion of merchandise, was arranged into seven departments: Silks, Embroideries, Furniture, Carpets, Porcelain, Curios, Miscellaneous. Not that these departments were spacious – the building was a warren of little rooms, mostly entered by archways knocked into dividing walls, or up separate flights of stairs. No more adjoining premises were available, but in 1883 Arthur Liberty was able to acquire a property further south on the same side of Regent Street, between Beak Street and Leicester Street. He named it Chesham House, in loyalty to his birthplace.

It was to be mainly devoted to carpets and furniture, and everything was trundled down by the staff in hand-trucks – William Judd recalled that this took 'some few weeks'. At first Chesham House consisted of a single shop, then the upper part of the next shop to the south was acquired, and later still the shop next but one to the north. A firm of jewellers, Rowlands and Frazer, occupied the premises between Liberty's two properties, so Liberty built a double staircase over the entrance to the jeweller's shop, making a humped passageway known to the staff as the Camel's Back. When Rowland and Frazer's lease lapsed, Liberty took over their shop, and Chesham House became the whole of 140–150 Regent Street.

But somewhere within their premises there was a Madame Louise, who remained an unmovable fixture. She, or rather the company she had founded, was described as 'the famous millinery undertaking with establishments in London, Paris, Biarritz and Monte Carlo'. Madame Louise originally seems to have pulled herself up to the West End by her bonnet strings. A. W. Foster in some recollections in the *Liberty Lamp* wrote: 'Rumour has it that Madame Louise the famous milliner, otherwise Mrs Thompson, migrated from Shoreditch, where she ran a business under the name of *The Bonnet Box*!' Mr Foster's exclamation mark conveys an innuendo that Mrs Thompson's 'Bonnet Box', like the 'friendly bonnet shop' of another Madame in the

42

Burlington Arcade mentioned in the *Survey of London,* was used for prostitution. But by whatever means Mrs Thompson raised the capital to move to Regent Street and become Madame Louise, there are no grounds for suspicion that her establishment there was not the height of respectability. It was still entrenched somewhere in the middle of Chesham House when the property was pulled down in 1924 at the rebuilding of Regent Street. At this juncture a company named Chesham House Ltd was formed in which Louise & Co. and Liberty owned all the issued shares. But Liberty's did not continue trading in Chesham House after the rebuilding.

In the basement of Chesham House there was an Eastern Bazaar. Here were Japanese and Chinese antiques, porcelain, bronzes, lacquer-ware, brass trays, Japanese dolls and fans, handscreens, antimony metalware, and a hotchpotch of things described as 'decorative furnishing objects' and 'miscellaneous Eastern knick-knacks'. A special attraction of the Bazaar was that it was illuminated by electric light. A little later the Arab Tea Room was opened on the First Floor, with a ladies' cloakroom . . . a rare convenience for shoppers in those days. There was no such consideration for the needs of gentlemen. Indian condiments could be bought in the Arab Tea Room: chutney, curry powder, Nepal pepper, Cayenne pepper, Guava jelly, Typaree jam. Also Indian and China tea, and jars of a preserved Chinese ginger particularly appreciated by epicures. These were included in the silk shipments 'to make up the weight'.

A special Curio Department was opened, where the connoisseur of the curious could browse amongst oriental armour, bronzes, and 'antique metalwork suitable for the decoration of halls, etc.'. Here were Japanese inlaid cabinets with rich decoration in ivory and pearl, Chinese carved blackwood furniture, fine specimens of antique blue-and-white porcelain and of antique enamel, early Chinese and Japanese pottery, lacquer, ivory, and carvings, swords, daggers, sabres and Kodsukse. A Modern China Department stocked Japanese, Satsuma, Kaga, and Imari vases, modern blue-and-white vases, and modern cloisonné enamel on copper.

Chesham House was neither more nor less convenient than East India House. One of the original staff there, J. T. Aggas, wrote of it in the *Liberty Lamp*:

'Shall we ever forget the many nooks and out-of-the-way corners and staircases, also the Camel's Back, an up-and-down stairway connecting the two houses, the mirrored walls that deceived staff and customers alike. How many humorous situations arose at seeing oneself reflected in so many ways! I remember an elderly dame apologising to her own mirror reflection, and craving pardon for her intrusion.'

Japanese Cloisonné Enamel vase, brilliantly enamelled on copper base; decoration of birds and flowers; 14 inches high, 5 gns. per pair, catalogue, 1883. Japanese Blue-and-white Tea Jar and Cover, 10 inches high, 5/–. Porcelain catalogue, 1883. Nankin Blue-and-white flower vase, Porcelain catalogue, c. 1880.

And Mr Roberts of the Furnishing and Decoration Studio recalled how when he arrived at Chesham House for the first time he was directed down a passage which proved to be no way through but simply 'a mirror cunningly draped with coloured Art muslins, then in vogue – an artifice far-sightedly introduced by the Founder to give the effect of extra spaciousness'. The reason he remembered this so well was because he walked straight into the mirror and damaged his nose. He recalled also that the Estate Agency Department was a small cabin or den just off the landing to the first floor, 'the manager being a very big man and out of all scale with the cabin'. The big man does not seem to have expanded the small department, for no references to Liberty & Co. as Estate and House Agents exist after the end of the century. Mr Roberts continued:

'A narrow and winding stair led to the upper floors, where were the studios, and above these were the polisher's shop and various store rooms. Telephones were then almost unknown, excepting a very crude system between the two houses, consisting of a single wire attached to a drum-like receiving box at each end, which you tapped to draw the attention of the person at the other end, and then you spoke your message. Speaking tubes were the only other means of communication, and the whistles blowing at frequent intervals from various departments had a most weird effect.'

In 1887 the 'Paper Hangings' were transferred from East India House to Chesham House to be near the Decoration Studio and put in the charge of William Judd. Mr Fletcher designed the 'Damasque' wallpapers in single prints. They sold in thousands of pieces. Later other papers were introduced, and a Liberty wallpaper book issued.

When Godwin wrote in *The Architect* that if only there was some decent furniture in the shop you could equip your whole house at Liberty's, it was all Japanese furniture of bamboo or lightweight lacquered wood. Gradually other furniture of Eastern manufacture was imported, mainly from Cairo ... Arab sideboards, wardrobes and writing tables. Then the new Furnishing and Decoration Studio was inaugurated under Mr Wyburd, described by Guy Bentley as 'a versatile and accomplished artist, who had made a profound study of Arabian design. A great feature of this style of decoration as applied to English furnishing, was the use of Moorish wooden arches with fretwork tracery across doorways and corridors, and it was a joke at Liberty's that "Mr Wyburd could draw them blindfold". They were very characteristic of "Liberty" décor, and the manager of the department said he sometimes saw representatives from rival firms making surreptitious sketches when the salesman's back was turned.'

The most fashionable example of the Arab vogue was Sir (later Lord) Frederick Leighton's house in Holland Park Road, now preserved as a museum. Osbert Lancaster tells in *An Eye for the Future* that at the outbreak of war in September 1939, Leighton House was used as an air raid warden's post, and describes the incongruity of the surroundings he, as a warden, found himself in when the first sirens sounded: 'The fountain in the pool in the Arab Hall tinkled irrelevantly, emphasising rather than breaking the silence; the squares of sunlight on the marble floor were cross-hatched by the patterns of the carved wooden grilles which covered every window; in the fretted squinches supporting the dome, gold-leaf gleamed in the bluish transmuted light reflected from the peacock tiles.'

In this milieu, Lord Leighton's guests, the artists and the aesthetes, the men of letters and dilettantes of Society, the pale and languid artists' models in their flowing dresses of Liberty silks, will have felt at one with their surroundings. It was a vogue which, unlike the Japanese mania, did not spread to Upper Tooting; but Moorish smoking rooms, if not Arab halls, were ordered by many Liberty customers. One of the earliest contracts on which the design studio worked was the music room of the Marquess of Aberdeen's house in Grosvenor Square, which was carried out in the oriental style with Moorish arches and panels used in conjunction with fine old tiles. About the same time, a rather similar scheme was carried out for the Lyric Club. During the winter of 1887, when Arthur Liberty and Emma Louise went to North Africa to see the Moorish scene for themselves, the firm re-decorated their house in Cornwall Terrace, Regent's Park. Sadly, no

Arab Smoking Room furnished by Liberty & Co. 'Brass hanging Mosque Lamp, Persian bronze dishes, antique brass repoussé and hand-engraved Incense Burners, antique metal Ewers.' Arab Musharabeyeh lattice (Mr Wyburd's speciality) in the background. Handbook of Sketches, 1890

record remains of the scheme of decoration they chose for that stronghold of the Regency. We only know from Emma Louise's journal that their house was not ready when they got back and they had to put up at an hotel ... 'A sad end to a fascinating trip,' she recorded. There will have been some ructions about that.

The outdoor representative of the Contracts Department for nearly forty years was Guy Bentley, an expert on interior decoration of all periods and styles. A classical scholar with literary leanings, he sometimes helped Arthur Liberty prepare the various papers he gave to learned societies. One of Guy Bentley's favourite recreations was book illumination, some of his work being shown at the Royal Academy. There is no doubt that Arthur Liberty had a genius for choosing men of many talents – and keeping them. Bentley was not in sympathy with either the Japanese style or the Arab. He wrote in the *Liberty Lamp*:

'Both had their run for a time and a very considerable trade was done in them, but they were after all exotics and could not flourish or be permanent in our climate and in the atmosphere of our traditions and national habits. The effort to produce "Japanese furniture" of bamboo combined with floor matting and lacquered or inlaid panels was always rather pathetic, as well as the manufacture of "Arab" sideboards, wardrobes and writing tables. These, I always said, were hopelessly incongruous, and at last the style came to be confined to the smoking lounge, for which it is well suited, combining as it does rich colour, subdued light, the quaint effect of Mushrabiyeh lattice, and luxurious divans and cushions.'

The bamboo furniture was made by a Monsieur Fortier, whose best and almost sole client was Liberty. With his hilarious English, he was a great favourite with the staff . . . 'Not more than 5 ft high, but sturdily built, with close-cropped white hair and white moustache and "imperial", a brown, whimsically good-looking face which seemed as though carved out of oak, he was a fine specimen of a typical French *pioupiou*. He had been a soldier in Algeria, was always light-hearted and merry, and habitually sang over his work: sometimes it was *Partant pour la Syrie,* sometimes *Marlbrouk s'en va t'en guerre.'*

A Scotsman named James Thallon was another individual character. He owned a cabinet factory, and by an arrangement with Liberty made furniture in their name, and acted as their representative. Liberty became his main customer, and about 1887 took over the workshops, James Thallon becoming an employee of the firm. His foreman was George Wolfe. With a shock of curly grey hair and pince-nez balanced precariously on the end of his nose, he was affectionately known as The Old Grey Wolfe. His pride of craftsmanship was such that when a contract was finished he wrote on the walls 'This work was fixed by George Wolfe of Liberty & Co.', and the date. When he retired, another member of the Contract Staff wrote in the *Liberty Lamp*: 'This wall writing will be found not only in the capitals of Europe, but also on many out of the way places on the Continent, and on the walls of houses

Bamboo Writing Bureau – 'front of drawer and writing flap beautifully lacquered, shelves and inside writing flap lined with gold leather paper. 65/-'

throughout the British Isles. If in the course of time work executed by George Wolfe is dismantled, and if the dismantler is himself a craftsman, he will assuredly say "A craftsman fixed this". George Wolfe became manager of the company's factories and after he had retired in 1925 his successor, Mr Pannell, asked the Board if he could consult him about a large purchase of autumn felled oak. And it was under the advice of The Old Grey Wolfe that Liberty & Co. made one of their largest ever purchases of "living" English oak.'

Arthur Liberty was at this time sympathetically involved with the Arts and Crafts Exhibition Society, initiated by Walter Crane, with the help of Lewis F. Day, the fabric and wallpaper designer, and J. D. Sedding, the architect and designer. The Society came into being when the Royal Academy had refused to consider including a decorative arts section in their annual summer exhibition. Some members of the Art Workers' Guild founded in 1884 were attracted, and by the time the first Arts and Crafts Exhibition was held in the New Gallery in the autumn of 1888, William Morris had joined. Burne-Jones became a member soon afterwards. The strength of the movement is indicated by the fact that the Society of Arts formed an 'Applied Arts' section at about this time.

The New Gallery superseded the Grosvenor Gallery that closed after a brilliantly fashionable ten years. Society had flocked to the evening receptions and Sunday afternoons given by Sir Coutts and Lady Lindsay. The most notable artists both within and without the Academy exhibited at the Grosvenor Gallery; but it began to be felt that the social side was becoming more important than the pictures. Walter Crane wrote: 'One heard that the frequent suppers and entertainments were distasteful to Burne-Jones, and it was even whispered that the labels announcing SOUPS and ICES were hung in front of some of his pictures.' Sir Coutts Lindsay's assistant directors, Comyns Carr and Charles Hallé, son of the famous pianist, resigned and started the New Gallery, transforming an abandoned meat market in Regent Street. Mrs Comyns Carr was reputed to be the original of du Maurier's Mrs Cimabue Brown. Virtually all the regular Grosvenor Gallery exhibitors went over to the New Gallery, and the Grosvenor soon closed. The building became a circulating library, then a club, and finally the Aeolian Hall, 'dedicated to the music of sweet sounds and the strains of the pianola'.

The catalogue of the first exhibition at the New Gallery contained various papers by members of the Art and Crafts Society; and lectures given at the gallery included one on tapestry and carpet weaving by William Morris. Charles Hallé arranged evenings when Isadora Duncan, his young protégée and inamorata at that time, danced after lectures by Sir William Richmond on 'Dancing in its relation to Painting', Andrew Lang on dancing and the Greek myth, and Sir Hubert Parry on dancing in relation to music. It was the time when Isadora, virtually penniless on her first visit to London with her brother, had gained a tenuous foothold by extracting an invitation to dance at a house in Grosvenor Square owned by an American hostess. In *My Life*, she relates that she also extracted ten pounds in advance, 'with which, after paying the rent of the studio, we bought some canned food as provision for the future, and I bought a few yards of veiling at Liberty's in which I appeared on Friday evening at Mrs X's party'. It was probably in the same few yards of Liberty veiling that she danced at the New Gallery.

Isadora also describes a dress she bought for an afternoon visit – 'A white muslin Kate Greenaway dress, which I wore with a blue sash under the arms and big straw hat on my head, and my hair in curls on my shoulders'. The 'Kate Greenaway dress' must surely have been bought in Liberty's children's department. And a little later she and her brother went to Paris and spent hours at the Louvre ... 'I have since met people who saw us there, me in my white dress and Liberty hat, and Raymond in his large black hat, open collar and flowing tie, and say we were two bizarre figures, so young and so absolutely absorbed in the Greek vases.'

Arthur Liberty's contact with the Arts and Crafts Society brought him many new friendships, and it is a pity that he was not, like so many of his contemporaries, either a diarist or a writer of the kind of letters people keep. He belonged to many societies, one of the less serious and more social being *Ye Sette of Odd Volumes*, of which he was President one year, as was his great friend and travelling companion Charles Holme, an editor of *The Studio*. Walter Crane described this gentlemen's dining club:

'Sometime in 1887 I was a guest at a dinner of "The Sette of Odd Volumes" – a dining club with a literary and artistic flavour, which used to meet once a month. The company was a large one, and the dinner long and elaborate. The *pièce de résistance*, however (outside the menu) was a paper by one of the members, followed by a discussion. The President of the year was called "His Oddship", and it was the odd custom for each "brother" to introduce his guest – describing him and his achievements, hitting off his peculiarities in a brief speech. I remember Oscar Wilde was present on one of these occasions, and pronounced an eulogy of Buffalo Bill who was rather a "lion" of the season when he and his cowboys first appeared on the wild prairies of Earl's Court. I first met Mr John Lane, the publisher, at the Odd Volumes.'

Membership was restricted to twenty-one, and candidates for election had to
have been guests at least twice. Arthur Liberty remained a member all his
life, and his nephew and heir Ivor Stewart-Liberty was elected after him.

Ye 272nd Meeting of
Ye Sette of Odd Volumes,
Held at Ye Imperial Restaurant (Oddenino's),
On Tuesday, ye 23rd day of October, 1906

DROPPING THE PILOT or 1905–06

Brother Lewis Boyd Sebastian, Skynner,
Becometh duly Installed in ye Chair in succession to
His Oddship, Brother A. Lasenby Liberty, Craftsman.

Menu for Ye Sette of Odd Volumes dinner on occasion of Liberty's
retirement from Presidency, October 23, 1906. Drawn by Jack
Hassall after the famous *Punch* cartoon by John Tenniel of Kaiser
Wilhelm dropping the pilot. Lewis Skynner's face for the Kaiser's,
Arthur Liberty for Bismarck

6

GODWIN AND THE COSTUME DEPARTMENT
ANTIQUE EMBROIDERIES

In 1884, the year after Chesham House was acquired, Arthur Liberty decided to open a Costume Department with its own studio and workrooms, where dresses would be designed and made in Liberty fabrics. It was an idea that shook some of the staff to the core, as Guy Bentley remembered:

'The establishment of the Costume Department was regarded by us all as a distinct break with the traditions of the Firm, and many felt uneasy at the introduction of Ladies' Costumes, with its concomitants of millinery and other phases of female adornment, into a business which was laying itself out for artistic decoration and the manufacture of articles and fabrics which would educate the public taste; it was felt that it would be difficult to keep out of the current of the whirling changes of fashion, and some doubted the wisdom of expecting men to give their patronage for furniture and decoration to an establishment where the feminine side of personal requirements was much in evidence.

'Although these doubts have not even now entirely disappeared [*Bentley is writing in 1931*] subsequent events have much modified them; and more especially when it was found that from the very beginning 'Liberty' Costumes were not to be influenced in the smallest degree by the ateliers of Paris.

'Broadly speaking, our designers have taken their models from historical costumes, modifying them for our own times and conditions, but always retaining something of the characteristic of the original. The designs for children's dresses, as shown in the books of Kate Greenaway, had already to some extent prepared the way; and soon it became very much the *mode* among artistic people and their imitators to wear a 'Liberty' gown at any special function – such was, in fact, recognisable at a glance. The introduction of the new department was made easier because from the earliest days of the Firm, garments from the East had formed part of the stock – such as Japanese kimonos, antique Chinese and Japanese embroidered coats and

51

robes, Turkish veilings and shoes. During the 1880s, we held annual exhibitions of embroideries, and the ladies of the Department used to don Circassian, Hindoo, Japanese and Chinese attire. But the success of the new department must be attributed to the Liberty fabrics. The ladies of my youth used to speak with admiration of silk dresses which "would stand alone"; but the designs of the Costume Department showed the beauty of soft draping lines, and this influence extended to the present day and has greatly modified the canons of good taste, both here and on the Continent.'

Success at the outset was also due to the publicity of having E. W. Godwin to direct the department. Arthur Liberty must surely be the only shopkeeper ever to have appointed a celebrated architect to supervise a dressmaking department. But then Arthur Liberty was no ordinary shopkeeper, and Edward Godwin's talents were far more versatile than those of an ordinary architect. Oscar Wilde once referred to Godwin as 'the greatest aesthete of them all'. Godwin had made a study of historic dress, and was Hon. Secretary of the Costume Society. He had written the handbook for the National Health Society Exhibition, advocating for modern dress the same principles as classic Greek costume. He and Arthur Liberty visualised the Costume Department as an educational, almost missionary project, the aim being 'to establish the craft of dressmaking upon some hygienic, intelligible and progressive basis; to initiate a renaissance that should commend itself artistically to leaders of art and fashion, and to challenge on its merits the heretofore all-powerful and autocratic fiat of Paris for "change" and "novelty" so far as it is oblivious of grace or fitness'. Godwin's knowledge of historic dress was invaluable 'for the study and execution of costumes embracing all periods, together with such modifications of really beautiful examples as may be adapted to the conventionalities of modern life without rendering them eccentric or bizarre'.

The formal letter of appointment still exists. Dated January 17, 1884, and addressed to E. W. Godwin, FSA, it confirms his appointment to supervise the Costume Department at a fee of one guinea for each hour engaged at the studio. The hours in any one week were not to exceed six hours, and 'each day shall be as is reasonable and practical'. In addition, he would have 'three-per cent on the gross amount of all orders received and executed in consequence of your personal introduction of clients'. Godwin's biographer, Dudley Harbron, writes in *The Conscious Stone* that he arranged private views for which mannequins were employed and the dresses were 'all worn by ladies whose stature and personal appearance was singularly in harmony with their style and dress'. These would almost certainly have been the ladies

ate Greenaway' dress with
ocked yoke and sleeves.
rtistic Dress for Children'
alogue, 1887

assic Greek gown 'Athene'
om *Liberty Art Costumes,*
87. In Arabian cotton with
k Himation.

of the Embroidery Department who used to don Circassian, Hindoo,
Japanese and Chinese attire when the annual exhibitions of embroideries
were held. There were no professional fashion models at this time, and
although the Pre-Raphaelite artists' models would have been ideal for the
Liberty dresses, it is most improbable that they would have condescended to
act as mannequins.

The appointment of Godwin was less than three years before his death in
October, 1886, years during which he was deeply involved with designing
for theatrical productions as well as with architectural commitments. We do
not know how long, or indeed how harmoniously, he worked in the dress
design studios, but his educational principles were still being advocated
when Liberty's catalogue of ART FABRICS AND PERSONAL SPECIALITIES for
1887 was issued:

'It is purposed to make a continued and systematic attempt to establish an
Educational School of Personal Adornment, where shall be secured such forms,
draperies, colours and ornaments as harmonise most perfectly with the
natural characteristics of the wearer; and where shall be provided, for

amateurs, artists and the stage, the most beautiful types of modern dresses, and the most reliable reproductions of ancient costume, plain or rich. We are indebted to Monsieur Chevreul's admirable work *The Laws of Contrast of Colour* for the following suggestions relating to Ladies' Dress, which will be found of great service in deciding upon the colours of a costume.'

There follow three pages of advice upon what shades should be worn by women of various skin and hair colouring. It is strange that there was no advice for women with red or auburn hair, the colour most admired by the Pre-Raphaelites and aesthetes. Earlier in the century, it had been considered a disaster for a girl to be afflicted with auburn hair, so it may be that M. Chevreul had not realised red heads had become all the rage. Mrs Haweis wrote in *The Art of Beauty* (1878):

'Morris, Burne-Jones, and others have made certain types of face and figure, once literally hated, actually the fashion. Red hair – once, to say a woman had red hair was social assassination – is all the rage. A pallid face with a protruding upper lip is highly esteemed. Green eyes, a squint, square eyebrows, whitey-brown complexion, are not left out in the cold. Now is the time for plain women. Only dress after the Pre-Raphaelite style, and you will be astonished to find that so far from being an "ugly duckling" you are a full-fledged swan.'

A bit sarcastic – Mrs Haweis herself probably had the pink and white complexion and blonde or raven tresses, that were being out-dated. A contributor to *Sylvia's Home Journal* in 1879 wrote less trenchantly but warningly on 'The Influence of Aesthetics on English Society': 'There is always a subtle charm in character more potent than that of simple prettiness . . . but there, however, begins the danger of aesthetics in dress – exaggeration, without a restraining taste. We have seen odd figures, with frizzled, dishevelled hair, distended sleeves, draggle-tail garments, wearing no dainty rim of white about neck or wrists.' The homely readers of *Sylvia's Home Journal* would probably prefer to model themselves on Society beauties than aesthetes, and the last thing they would wish to be mistaken for would be an artist's model.

Monsieur Chevreul's advice in Liberty's catalogue was followed by drawings of 'Liberty Art Costumes': A Grecian costume in Arabian Cotton; a caped mantle in Himalaya Cashmere, lined with Liberty Silk; a peasant dress in thin Umritza Cashmere, embroidered and smocked; a Cashmere Tea Gown, flowing and droopy, silk embroidered at neck and waist. It concluded with

Teagowns by Liberty in typical
Liberty furnished room. From
the *Lady's World*, July, 1887

four pages of 'Artistic Dress for Children', all with the Kate Greenaway
look, smocking at waist, or neck and cuffs. Sarah Bernhardt brought her
grandchild to be fitted.

Kate Greenaway's influence on children's clothes, reviving the style of the
early 1800s, was extraordinary. It began with the publication in 1878 of
Under the Window, engraved and printed by the incomparable Edmund
Evans, who did beautiful work for children's books by Randolph Calde-
cott and Walter Crane. *Under the Window* sold well in America, and was
issued in German, French, and Belgian editions. Two years later the original
drawings for the book were exhibited at the Fine Art Society. She was compared with Stothard, praised by the critics, most particularly by Ruskin.
When in 1883 the first *Kate Greenaway Almanack* appeared, it sold 90,000
copies in England, America, France, and Germany, and was succeeded by an
Almanack every year (except 1896) until 1897. Through the medium of these
Almanacks it was said 'she dressed the children of two continents'. One of
Kate Greenaway's great admirers was Arthur Liberty, although it is unlikely
he would go as far as John Ruskin who, in praising one of her Christmas
cards, wrote: 'To my mind it is a greater thing than Raphael's St Cecilia.'
One must take into account that this was not a published estimation, but was

SKETCH-DESIGN FOR THE PLATE AFFIXED ABOVE THE KATE GREENAWAY COT IN THE GREAT ORMOND STREET HOSPITAL.
Designed by Mrs. Arthur Lasenby Liberty.

in a 'fan letter' to Kate Greenaway before he had met her. Nevertheless, Ruskin remained besotted with her work all his life, although deploring her inability to draw feet, reprimanding her for having no sense of form, begging her (in vain) to make studies from the nude . . . 'As we've got so far as taking off hats, I trust we may in time get to taking off just a little more – say, mittens – and then – perhaps – even – shoes – and (for fairies) even stockings – and – then – .'

Her biographers, M. H. Spielmann and G. S. Layard, suggest that she 'introduced a Pre-Raphaelite spirit into the art of the nursery'; and Arthur Liberty, himself such an admirer of the Pre-Raphaelites, was quoted by *The British Warehouseman* in 1895 as saying he admired Kate Greenaway 'as being one of the earliest and most powerful popular educators in my colour theories with her simple little outline drawings'. When she died in 1902, he was the honorary treasurer of a Kate Greenaway Memorial fund committee. With the money raised a Kate Greenaway cot was endowed at the Great Ormond Street Hospital for Children, and the plate fixed above it was designed by Emma Louise Liberty.

*   *   *   *   *

An American journalist called Annie Wakeman visited the Costume Department in January, 1884, when it was first opened at 7 Argyll Street, and this is how she described it in the *British and Mercantile Gazette*:

'The reception room of itself is a study. To enter this room rests one instantly, it looks so sweet and quiet and full of harmony. Several young ladies spend their entire time in getting up new designs adapted from classic models. For the taste of today there must be a clinging under-dress, fitted perfectly, of silk, velvet or cashmere. About this, soft drapings are arranged, suited to the figure of the wearer. The everlasting and monotonous rows of frills and pleats are thus done away with, and garments substituted which have a meaning and subtlety of their own.'

When this journalist writes of 'the taste of today' she is referring to the taste of the aesthetes, which was by no means that of the majority of women in the 1880s, who were tightly corseted in stiff silken dresses with prominent bustles. From the Costume Department she went on to the main shop in Regent Street: 'It is as inappropriate to regard Liberty's merely as a place of business as it would be to regard the public library of Boston merely as a storage house of books. Both in their way are distinct institutions, and Liberty & Co. is as much a feature of the metropolis as the National Gallery or the Grosvenor Gallery. This sumptuous establishment, or rather establishments, for there are three or four, is crowded daily to the utmost capacity of its 34 or 35 beautiful rooms, as well as its main shop. It is a positive art education to stroll through these treasure-trove receptacles.'

She enthused over carpets, fabrics, jewellery, enamel work, jade, china, pottery, handwoven rugs, tapestries, wrought ironwork. She commented on 'cabinets of elaborate wood carving and screens of the most marvellous designs, real peacocks' feathers, and elaborate raised flowers'. And she reported that 'one innovation rapidly gaining favour is the substitution of carved wood window panels for stained glass – the effect is that of lattice-work'. Mr Wyburd and his famous Moorish screens at work! She reported also that 'a great interest has sprung up in Eastern embroideries, and Liberty have imported the peculiar silk skeins and gold thread that will no doubt start a charming new departure in fancy needlework for feminine fingers'.

The interest in Eastern embroideries was partly due to the Russo-Turkish war. When the refugees poured into Constantinople, a Turkish Compassionate Fund was set up to organise the sale of silk and gold Turkish embroideries worked by the refugee women. Lady Layard and Mrs Arthur Hanson were the organisers in Constantinople, and Lady Burdett-Coutts

urkish ✤ Embroidery.❉

SAMPLES FOR BORDERING FOR WHICH ORDERS CAN BE EXECUTED IN CONSTANTINOPLE.

and Lady Charlotte Schreiber in London. Liberty & Co. acted as agents for the embroiderers, holding displays of their work for sale in the shop. Orders for dress lengths with special borderings to be executed in Constantinople were handled by the firm.

Liberty's ransacked Europe and the East for antique embroideries, as well as commissioning contemporary work. A catalogue of 'a valuable and unique collection of ancient and modern, Eastern and Western, ART EMBROIDERIES at Chesham House in April, 1894', contains descriptions of nearly two hundred items. It includes an 'antique Italian Altar Frontal, a unique example of the early sixteenth century, taken by a French officer during the occupation of Rome by Napoleon in 1797'. There were specimens of Kin-Kob, or Cloth of Gold . . . 'the use of precious metals in the weaving of fabrics is of great antiquity, and extensively used today by the Maharajas and Rajahs of India. Kin-Kob is probably the most gorgeous material ever used for human apparel'. There were Portuguese Jewish altar frontals, temple hangings from Japan and Baluchistan, sixteenth-century Genoese chasubles, Turkish portières, antique Flemish tapestry panels, French, Spanish and Italian brocades, embroideries from Armenia, Persia, Anatolia, Java, China. Also on display, a specimen of an Eastern tobe 'Made by Messrs. Liberty for exportation to Africa. Used by traders as presents to the native chiefs'.

This embroidery exhibition included some examples of tie-and-dye work . . . 'known as Kamalka Tuks, the method is very primitive and curious. The cloth is doubled and then gathered up into little knots, which are tied so tightly that the dye cannot penetrate them. After dipping in the dye, each knot is untwisted, when a quaint design appears. Many experienced officers in India wear these cloths during the rainy season, as wet will not penetrate them. They are sold by the Bainas in the Bazaars of Jeypore'. It will be remembered from Chapter 2 that Edward Godwin used a similar method, although tie-and-dry instead of tie-and-dye, to produce a crinkled clinging effect for Ellen Terry's dress as Titania.

A catalogue of 1887 includes 'shawls from the valley of Cashmere, the finest specimens of needlework known . . . the fabric is "built-up" with minute pieces arranged in such a manner as to form designs of striking beauty'. Prices of these were from £30 to £500. Less expensive were the Dacca shawls of similar but much coarser workmanship. There were Delhi shawls, suitable for carriage wraps, embroidered in floss silk with bold designs; Rampoor Chuddah shawls; Tunisian wraps in silk and wool stripes. There were also howdah cloths, embroidered in gold – failing an elephant, they made magnificent carriage rugs.

7

DECORATING CONTRACTS; PLAGIARISM
PARIS BRANCH

The services of the Contracts Department at Chesham House were in great demand during the eighties. Charity bazaars in aid of worthy causes were a recurring feature of Victorian high society life, and Liberty's were often called upon to transform the ugly public buildings in which they were usually held. They would fix wall hangings and tent-like ceilings. And, as a member of the Contract Staff put it, 'the draping of a stall or a window with Liberty Silk, or palampores, or phulkaris, gave scope to much artistic taste in form and colour'.

Exhibitions, also, were fashionable – symbolic of the earnest culture of the Victorians and of their pride in Britain's industry and her Empire. During the eighties, four major exhibitions were held in the old grounds of the Albert Hall, the site of the future Indian Museum. There were the Fisheries Exhibition, the Health Exhibition, the Inventions Exhibitions, and the Colonial and Indian Exhibitions – in all of which Liberty's participated. One would hardly expect them to be at the Fisheries Exhibition (1883), at which exhibits from all over the world were assembled to illustrate fishing methods. But 'as the preparations advanced, the exhibition began to include many kinds of manufacture totally unconnected with fishing. For instance, Liberty & Co. made a brave show of antiques and other oriental goods. Mr B. Blake was engaged to take charge of our stand, a man whose knowledge of these goods was extensive and peculiar'.

Mr Blake was afterwards retained by Liberty's as buyer of the Oriental Antiques and Curios Department. Having been for many years connected with Chinese trade in Mincing Lane, he introduced to his department Guava jelly and other edible products of the Far East that could scarcely be described as antiques, but possibly as curios. Customers were amused to see him with a row of small teapots and cups, infusing and tasting tea.

The most taxing undertaking was the Indian village set up at the Albert Palace in Battersea Park in November, 1885. The Albert Palace was a glass

and iron building, similar to the Crystal Palace. It was first erected for a
national exhibition in Dublin, and later transported to Battersea Park. A
grand organ was installed, there were stalls selling knick-knacks, reading
and smoking rooms, a picture gallery, refreshment rooms, and kitchens
capable of cooking for 50,000 people. It was opened in June, 1885, by the
Lord Mayor, a flourish of trumpets, and a dedicatory ode composed by Mr
A. J. Caldicott; in the evening there were illuminations and fireworks.

For the Indian Village, the Albert Palace Association asked Liberty & Co.
to be responsible for bringing over a contingent of Indian natives, and Mr A.
Bonner was 'entrusted with the duty of collecting them in India, and
personally superintending their passage to England'. The heroism of Mr
Bonner, the tact that he must have exercised, can be realised by studying a
printed list in the Liberty archives that gives details of his thirty natives.
Their religions were Hindoo, Mahomedan, Roman Catholic, and Zhurthos-
thi; they represented no less than twenty different castes. The skills for
which they had been chosen included those of silk spinners, saree weavers,
Bijapoor carpet weavers, embroiderers, inlaid box makers, furniture carvers,
Poonah figure makers and dressers, beetle wing embroiderers. There was a
Kutch silver worker and engraver, a sandal-wood carver, a pottery painter,
a sitah and seringhi maker. The entertainers were: a dancing boy, a snake
charmer and juggler, a singing and dancing master, knife juggler, dancing
girls, acrobats. There were three musicians: Tabaljee, Tum Tum Chokra,
and Siringhi Vallah; and three cooks: Mahomedan, Brahmin, and Hindoo.
Their names ranged from something simple like Wittoba Ganoo to com-
plications such as Sayad Mahomed Valud Fatti Mahomed.

A note at the foot of the printed list says, 'Sir Frank Sonbar of Bombay,
in his official capacity, gave most valuable aid. But the fact of such various
Indian Castes being associated together is unprecedented, and the difficulties
surmounted can perhaps only be fully appreciated by Anglo-Indians.' Brave
Mr Bonner, Anglo-Indian or not, must have fully appreciated the difficulties
before the long voyage was ended. One must spare a thought also for the
Indians arriving in England in November. There is no record of how they
returned. Sir Edward Lee, Chairman of the Albert Palace Company, explained the somewhat optimistic object of the undertaking at a reception for
the Indians at the Mansion House. 'It was to facilitate the manufactures of
this country by showing what could be done in India by natives with their
own appliances.'

Other exhibitions in the eighties in which Liberty's participated were held
at the Aquarium, Westminster, at the Indian Museum, and at the Art
Needlework School in South Kensington. They themselves held an exhibi-

tion of Japanese works of art over Hengler's Circus in Argyll Street, for which they set up a complete Japanese house. The most attractive occasion was the Silver Fête at South Kensington in 1888, held to celebrate the twenty-fifth anniversary of the wedding of the Prince of Wales and Princess Alexandra. The previous year was Queen Victoria's Golden Jubilee. William Judd recalled the preparations:

'Regent Street was profusely decorated with flowers, beflagged and illuminated at night, when Londoners first saw the full power of the electric light which, although no longer a novelty, had never been seen on such a scale. Liberty's were called on to carry out decorations for other firms as well as their own buildings at East India House and Chesham House. I was sent with a cabful of red and white dhurries to the *Daily Chronicle* office in Fleet Street, where I draped twelve windows (by myself) working right through the night. When I arrived at Regent Street at six o'clock in the morning, I was let in for helping to decorate the front of the house with palampores. Was I tired? Not half! However, it was all life and excitement, so I did not mind.'

One of India's richest native princes was spending the winter of 1887–8 at Brighton, and a grand ball was given at the Pavilion. For assignments on this scale, Liberty's used to sub-contract the carpentry work to a firm of ball furnishers; Liberty upholsterers then added the draperies and other decorations. Guy Bentley led the Liberty team:

'Several truck loads of carpets, rugs, embroideries, palampores and other oriental goods valued at over £2,000 were transported to Brighton, and in about forty-eight hours the Pavilion was transformed into a scene from the Arabian nights. Our immediate client throughout was the wife of the British Resident at the Rajah's Court, who acted as hostess, and she took care to provide us with necessary refreshment, in the shape of an excellent dinner at 5 o'clock in the evening.'

Mr Bentley and his two colleagues were invited to attend the ball and . . .

'having sent home for our warpaint, we took our places at 8 o'clock with the other guests to line the procession. Shortly after the Prince appeared with his suite, his hostess on his arm. His poor Rani was concealed in a small room fitted up for her where, behind Musharabeyeh screens, she could watch the festivities.

'It was a brilliant pageant, the magnificent dresses of the Rajah and his

Indian ✦ Pyjamas. ❋

Libertys' soft Indian Silks are specially adapted for Pyjamas, being exquisitely soft, very light, durable, and of excellent washing qualities.

✦ Plain, White, Cream or Art Colours. ✦

PATTERNS AND INSTRUCTIONS FOR MEASUREMENT POST FREE.

Catalogue of 1883

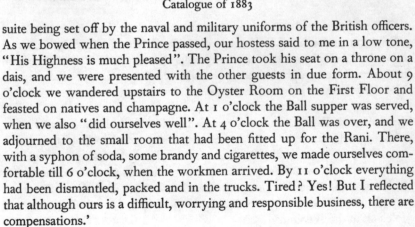

suite being set off by the naval and military uniforms of the British officers. As we bowed when the Prince passed, our hostess said to me in a low tone, "His Highness is much pleased". The Prince took his seat on a throne on a dais, and we were presented with the other guests in due form. About 9 o'clock we wandered upstairs to the Oyster Room on the First Floor and feasted on natives and champagne. At 1 o'clock the Ball supper was served, when we also "did ourselves well". At 4 o'clock the Ball was over, and we adjourned to the small room that had been fitted up for the Rani. There, with a syphon of soda, some brandy and cigarettes, we made ourselves comfortable till 6 o'clock, when the workmen arrived. By 11 o'clock everything had been dismantled, packed and in the trucks. Tired? Yes! But I reflected that although ours is a difficult, worrying and responsible business, there are compensations.'

Well might he so reflect. And there was also satisfaction . . .

'The local papers that week were filled with descriptions of the Ball, that of the decorations alone occupying four columns. Such a function as this can never recur, since after the frightful holocaust of the Paris Bazaar thirty years ago [*he is writing in 1927*], the law was enacted that all decorations for entertainments in public buildings must be fireproofed – and this, of course, renders it impossible for any but the cheapest material to be employed.'

The price of success is plagiarism. There had been attempts, it will be remembered, to copy Umritza Cashmere; and when Liberty introduced and made fashionable a particular kind of soft silk handkerchief in 'Liberty' natural dyes, they soon found that 'imitators have sprung up, and have succeeded so far in copying the colours, by the aniline process, that many at first sight might be misled. Therefore, to protect their patrons and avoid error, Liberty & Co. now stamp all their artistic-dyed handkerchiefs with their special registered LOTUS BRAND, without which none are genuine'. Protests were also made against 'the practices of certain piratical manufacturers and shopkeepers who, as destitute of originality as of commercial honesty, copy our cloths in inferior yarns and fugitive colours, which they offer as LIBERTY FABRICS and in some cases at a lower price than the genuine goods cost to produce. The LIBERTY ART FABRICS are our exclusive speciality, and can only be obtained at our Regent Street houses, or through duly accredited Country Agents'.

By 1887, pirating had reached actionable proportions. Liberty put in an application in the High Court before Mr Justice North on February 12th, 1887, to restrain the defendants, the Junior Army & Navy Stores Limited, from selling silk squares and silk sashes as of the plaintiffs' manufacture. A perpetual injunction was granted. The Junior Army & Navy was formed in 1879 by a breakaway group from the original Army & Navy Stores in Victoria Street. They had an imposing six-storey building, York House, in Waterloo Place. It looked like a gentleman's club, but in fact sold everything expected of a department store, as well as providing hairdressing departments for ladies and gentlemen, cloakrooms, and what were probably the first two passenger lifts in a London shop.

In France, the term '*soie Liberty*' had come into general use for any softly draping 'Art Silk' whether genuine Liberty or a French fabric of a similar type. At the *Exposition Universelle* in 1889, Liberty's exhibited some aesthetic gowns designed and made in their Costume Department. The orders taken were encouraging, so premises were acquired at 38 avenue de l'Opéra, and in April, 1890, a handsome two-colour circular on parchment-type paper announced:

'*Les créations de la Maison* "LIBERTY" *ont fait courir tout Paris au moment de l'Exposition Universelle; et c'est pour répondre au désir exprimé par ses nombreux clients, qu'elle s'est décidée à établir une succursale à Paris qui est ouverte depuis quelques semaines.*

Messieurs LIBERTY & CIE *ont tenu à soumettre à la critique Parisienne les spécimens les plus remarquables de leur créations uniques, et une visite à leur*

*établissement ne peut être que très intéressante pour toute dame ayant le souci de
la toilette élégante.'*

Stanford Griffin, a cousin of Arthur Liberty's, went from East India House
to be manager of the Paris branch, taking some staff with him; but the
workroom personnel were recruited in Paris. The windows were draped in
Liberty Art Fabrics, and in the salon a couture collection was shown of
models based on classical costume. But all was by no means *cordiale*. It was
reported in the *Draper's Record* that 'for some time the staff was in actual
physical danger, and had to be protected by the police. The house itself was
threatened to be burnt. And, amazing as it seems, the ground of complaint
was that in producing their goods the firm had stolen the brains of French
workmen, and were using them solely to the advantage of the foreigner'.

However, Liberty's kept their foothold. They established friendly rapport
with the French staff, a French manager was soon appointed to replace Mr
Griffin, and a good deal of cordial interchange went on between the staff at
Regent Street and in the avenue de l'Opéra. According to the *British
Warehouseman*, the Maison Liberty became 'the centre of a Parisian social
craze for Liberty costumes and decoration, which is spreading every day'.
A particular attraction was the Children's Salon, specialising in smocking
and Kate Greenaway dresses. At the 1889 *Exposition* the British section had
included thirteen frames of drawings by Kate Greenaway; and among the
many tributes paid by French art critics was that of Ernest Chesneau:
'*Lancés au milieu d'une société blasée, ces échappés de nurseries, vêtus à la mode
bizarre et charmante qu'on appelle maintenant "la Greenaway", était à coup
sûr original.'* The nursery escapes at the Exhibition, together with the French
editions of the *Kate Greenaway Almanacks*, led to it becoming mandatory for
all chic little Parisiennes to be dressed at the Maison Liberty.

Naturally the Costume Department in Regent Street benefited by reflected
kudos from the Paris branch. A catalogue issued in 1892 announced a revival
of the Empire style, with gowns by Parisian modistes made from Liberty Art
Fabrics. 'Messrs Liberty are able to offer to their clients the advantage of a
prior and careful study of the Empire mode acquired by some years of
experience in designing and fitting for Parisian Clients.' The catalogue
included original sketches dated May, 1813, of Empire Walking Gowns and
evening dresses. Customers calling at East India House would be shown a
selection of made-up models, and also accurate studio sketches culled from
eighteenth-century manuscripts and other reliable sources.

By the end of the century, there were about a hundred employees at the
Maison Liberty. Ferdinand David, who was for more than twenty years in

the Delivery Service, recalled in the *Liberty Lamp* how he pedalled around Paris on his tricycle, 'a box mounted on three wheels – at the sharp turnings these little vehicles threatened to overturn. The large firms also had fine carriages drawn by horses and made deliveries "*hors des fortifications*". I remember one, a good natured fat coachman, with florid complexion, wearing a high hat, very glossy. He often wore sabots, especially in winter. His vocabulary was graphic and amusing, interspersed with slang. He was a faithful customer of the wine merchants and knew what was good'. Monsieur David also remembered the three-horse omnibuses which plied in Paris in the 1890s as they did in London. Some of Liberty's deliveries were made by omnibus, and 'the customers paid in gold, never by cheque'.

In London, the Liberty vans were chocolate colour. William Ginger was in charge of the much admired pair-horse van for twenty-three years from 1890. When the inevitable change from horse to motor vehicles came, a member of the staff recalled, 'Our old friend with undaunted courage took to the new type of driving like a duck to water, and in a few weeks he was a proficient chauffeur, a calling that is also followed by his three sons. In 1919 he was awarded the Safety First Medal in the Freedom from Accidents Competition, and at the age of sixty-eight he continues to be a most reliable motor man.'

Before going to open the Paris house, Stanford Griffin had in 1887 opened a Liberty branch at 117–19 Corporation Street, Birmingham, which later moved to 43 New Street. Other towns and cities in the British Isles had Liberty agents. A list of 1890 gives the names of shops in Aberdeen, Bournemouth, Dover, Dublin, Edinburgh, Glasgow, Leeds, Liverpool, Manchester, Scarborough, Taunton, Torquay. There were also agents in far away places: in New York, Boston, Chicago, Toronto and Tasmania. In Shanghai, Arts & Crafts Ltd, Complete House Furnishers, were Sole Agents for Liberty & Co.; and in Japan, some proud agent produced a badly printed CURIO CATALOGUE with no name or address on it except: LIBERTY'S OF LONDON, PARIS, and YOKOHAMA.

Liberty's first Registered Trade Mark

8

INTO THE NINETIES; THE PUBLIC COMPANY
THE PEDIGREE

In 1887 Arthur Liberty took a partner. He needed someone to be at the helm temporarily, because he was planning a voyage round the world for the following year, accompanied by Sir Alfred East, RA, and Charles Holme. At a staff dinner to celebrate Queen Victoria's Jubilee, it was announced that Mr Frank Brunton Goodyer had been admitted to partnership. Early next year two other directors were appointed, William Street and John William Howe, who had been Arthur Liberty's private secretary since 1884. They were not given any financial stake in the business, and the partnership of Mr Goodyer was dissolved in 1889. According to one account, he had been importing vast quantities of silk from the East without advising the Counting House when his bills would be coming due, with resulting financial chaos. He departed to set up his own fabric business in Bond Street, naming it 'The Aesthetic Gallery for Art Fabrics', specialising in English silks, cashmeres, and velveteens.

In 1889 John Llewellyn joined the Silk Department from Howell & James. An exceptionally gifted young Welshman, he had come to London to train as a singer. His singing teacher mistakenly tried to make a tenor of him, trained his voice too high, and ruined it. Frustrated in his choice of a career, Llewellyn nevertheless determined to stay in London where all that was most important in music and the arts was happening; and when he saw a vacancy advertised at Howell & James, he thought it would give him a foothold and a small salary while he looked around. Like most creative people, he had an extremely nervous temperament; and by the time he arrived at the staff entrance to apply for the vacancy, he was in such a state that instead of ringing the doorbell he rang the fire bell. The whole of the staff came rushing down the back stairs, including the Managing Director. Smelling no smoke and suspecting a hoax, he demanded, 'Who rang that alarm?' 'I did, Sir,' answered the trembling Llewellyn. 'And why, may I ask?' 'I wanted to apply for the post.' 'Oh, you did, did you! Well, anyone who rings the fire

66

Harold Blackmore   John Llewellyn

alarm to apply for a post gets it.' And he was hired to start the next day. No fire bells were rung at Liberty's on the day he joined them, but in retrospect his arrival can be seen to have been a momentous one for the firm. His appointment was another proof that Arthur Liberty had an instinct for the right man. Someone else had an instinct about this also: Mr Nelrood, the buyer of the Silk Department. Before long he went to the Chairman and told him he had a really brilliant young man under him whom he could not hold down, so he thought it would be best if he were to retire. And he did. So in 1891 John Llewellyn was appointed head of the Silk Department, buyer in chief of the most important side of the business. The department buyers in those days were dictators of all they surveyed, and behaved like autocrats. Llewellyn was a very handsome young man, who dressed like an artist but with a touch of the dandy. He was also an enthusiast with the power to transmit his enthusiasm to those who trained under him, and to give the salesmen in the shop a real appreciation of the fabrics they handled. He was responsible for the commission and purchase of designs, for the liaison with Littler's hand-block printworks at Merton, and with all the firms who undertook weaving, dyeing, and machine printing for Liberty. It was through John Llewellyn that Alexander Morton used the Liberty shop as the first market place for his famous 'fadeless' dyes.

Liberty's determination to work in co-operation with industrialists and scientists, his belief that the aesthetically acceptable could be combined with the commercially viable, was applauded by Norman Shaw. Shaw was not only the most fashionable architect of the Aesthetic Movement, but also an RA, a designer of furniture for the joinery firm of W. H. Lascelles, and a partner in the firm of J. Aldam Heaton, makers of furniture, carpets, wallpaper, stained glass, embossed leatherwork. He wrote to Arthur Liberty:

'Yes, you have put your mark on your time – like Pugin, Whistler, and fortunately some others. You found things – most of 'em beastly – and you leave them glorious in colour and full of interest. What more could you desire? It is the fashion nowadays to run down Commercialism; but I don't see it – it is only when Commercialism is bad, and associated with bad Art, that it is objectionable; in other respects it is good and right, and a good backbone. Go on and prosper: and the longer you go on, and the more you prosper, the better for Art.'

By the final decade of the century, Arthur Liberty had developed from being a talented young man anticipating artistic trends and influencing fashions – an impresario of decorative arts – into an almost Establishment figure. In 1890 he was forty-seven years old, which was 'getting on' in Victorian times. He was certainly too old to be *dans le vent* of the decadent nineties. Aestheticism had taken on a green-carnation artificiality, an intellectual dandyism, a world-weary cynicism. There was a pursuit of perverse sensations, a search for romance in exhaustion and excess. *Fin de siècle* had become a modish phrase. Oscar Wilde was at the peak of his fame as a playwright; and a new generation of young men were exciting the artistic and literary coteries, notably Aubrey Beardsley, Max Beerbohm, Arthur Symonds, and William Rothenstein. The first issue of *The Studio* in 1893 introduced many fresh talents inside its Beardsley cover; while in the following year *The Yellow Book* began its short existence. The names that mattered now were not the names of the aesthetic seventies and eighties. Rossetti and Godwin were dead, Charles Keene died in the first year of the nineties; Ruskin was a sick man of over seventy; Leighton, Watts, and the leading Pre-Raphaelites – Millais, Ford Madox Brown, Holman Hunt, Burne-Jones – had all achieved a sober age. Kate Greenaway, in a letter written to John Ruskin in 1896, asked his opinion of Aubrey Beardsley's drawings . . . 'A great many people,' she wrote, 'are now what they call modern. When I state my likes and dislikes they tell me I am *not* modern. So I suppose I'm not – advanced. You must not like Leighton now, or Millais, and I don't know how much longer I'm allowed to like Burne-Jones. Oh dear!'
    Arthur Liberty was now a member of the Society of Arts, and in 1890 had

Arthur Liberty in the 'Trial Studio' with John Llewellyn, William Street, and J. W. Howe

received its Silver Medal for a paper on *The Industrial Arts and Manufactures of Japan* – he would receive another Silver Medal in 1900 for his paper on *English Furniture*. He was a member of the Royal Institute, Fellow of the Asiatic Society, member of the Organising Council of the Japan Society, Fellow of the Royal Historical Society, the Royal Statistical Society, the Zoological Society, a member of the Council of the London Chamber of Commerce, a director of the British Produce Supply Association, Master of the Glass Sellers' Company, Vice-President of the Silk Association of Great Britain and Ireland, President of the English Monumental Inscription Society. Of short stature, he was now a little portly, and wore a dignified beard. He was gratified at being mistaken for the Prince of Wales. This happened quite often, especially when travelling abroad, for he bore a striking resemblance to the heir to the throne.

A reference to this likeness occurs in some recollections by A. W. Foster, in which he relates how he used to take a selection of Christmas gifts for inspection by the Princess of Wales (later Queen Alexandra) at Marlborough House:

'Silverware and Chuddah shawls especially appealed to the Princess, and her purchases usually totalled up to £70 or £80. The large Drawing-room overlooking the lawn was used for the display, with trestle tables brought in. But on one occasion it was in use for another purpose, and we had to make our display in a first-floor bedroom. We were merrily pinning our scarves and draperies to the four posts of the bed when Miss Charlotte Knollys, the Lady in Waiting, looked in and saw with horror our array of drawing pins. However, just then the fragrance of a wonderful cigar and the appearance from the corridor of the Prince of Wales saved the situation. His voice, manner and profile were replicas of those of our Founder, whom he resembled in many ways: the soft, ingratiating voice, the "calm before a storm".'

From other recollections we know that the storms blew up very swiftly. There was, for example, Mr Elsom's experience:

'In the early days Mr L. was very fond of coming into Chesham House and asking a question of the first man he met. He would say, "How much cash have you taken today, Mr Elsom?" I had been busy serving, how on earth was I to know, so I would say, "Well, Sir, I think about – ." He would say, "I don't want you to think, but to know, and not how many wells or rivers you have, but how much cash you have taken." So I would say, "I will find out," and he would say, "I don't want you to find out, of course it's left to me to do that, why don't you say you don't know?"'

For some time various members of the Liberty family had been trying to trace their origin. The search for a pedigree was a very popular late-Victorian pursuit – it was not only du Maurier's Sir Gorgius Midas who was digging around to find ancestors' graves. Culleton's Heraldic Library, when consulted, gave the derivation of the English name Liberty as 'Leadbeater', and traced a Scottish Liberty family whose name derived from a locality in Fife; also an American family descended from an ancestor who changed his name to Liberty at the Declaration of Independence. The *Patronymica Britannica* revealed a leather-merchant Liberty whose son Jonathan Liberty, born 1794, was apprenticed to a glass-cutter of Shoe Lane in the City of London. He moved to Blackfriars where his son, Jonathan Richard Liberty, also became a glass-cutter, at one time working for the famous Whitefriars Ecclesiastic Glass House of Powell & Co. Another line of research in Buckinghamshire revealed Liberty marriages in the church register at Chalfont St Giles in 1716, and at Chalfont St Peter in 1722; while at Kensworth in Bedfordshire, the first record of many Libertys was found to be in 1619. Daniel Liberty, a yeoman farmer who died at Kensworth in 1815, had three sons; one became a breeches-maker at Luton, one became a carpenter at Weybridge, and the third became a wheelwright at Chesham, where Arthur Lasenby Liberty's father had his draper's shop.

But meanwhile Arthur Lasenby Liberty himself was on the scent of a much more romantic trail, which led him in 1886 to Marseilles city library, from whence he returned home with this story: A Corsican named Pierre Baglioni was the leader of a successful conspiracy to free his native town of Calvi from the Spanish yoke, attacking with the cry of 'Liberti, Liberti!' His grateful fellow citizens gave him the surname Libertà. Later, his descendants emigrated to Marseilles; and it was a Pierre de Libertat who led the citizens to defend the port against the Spaniards. For this he was ennobled by Henry of Navarre, and permitted to show the fleur-de-lis upon his arms. At the French Revolution the de Libertat family sought refuge in England. They became British nationals and anglicised the name to Liberty.

As Horace Walpole wrote in his *Detached Thoughts*, 'History is a romance that is believed; romance, a history that is not believed' . . . a peculiarly relevant epigram in our context, since Walpole also observed, 'There is a probability that I am descended from Chaucer' – and followed it by adding, 'Mr Chute says anybody with two or three hundred years of pedigree may find themselves descended from whom they please.' Well, it pleased Arthur Liberty to find himself descended from the romantic Pierre de Libertat. He had de Libertat armorial ensigns and crest traced in the Marseilles city library and in 1898 obtained a grant of arms from Her Majesty's Garter Principal King of Arms, and armorial ensigns duly recorded to the Liberty family in the College of Heralds. And by the time this pursuit of a pedigree had come to such a satisfactory conclusion, he had altered his life style to match his escutcheon by going to live at The Lee Manor in Buckinghamshire, four miles from his birthplace Chesham, and even nearer the village of Chartridge where his mother's family, the Lasenbys, had lived since the seventeenth century.

Things have a meaning when they come at the right moment; and at the moment when Arthur Liberty heard through the Lasenbys that the Manor was to let many things apart from the pedigree may have combined to influence his decision. He had already appointed two directors to help run the business, and was contemplating making the firm into a public company. He and Emma Louise had no children, and her life in the handsome house in fashionable Regent's Park could have been lonely. His professional contacts and varied interests had won him the entrée into intellectual circles, but most of these were masculine. She would be happier in the country. Members of the Plaistowe family had been Lords of the Manor of The Lee and Patrons of the Living since the seventeenth century; but the house itself had been occupied for many years by a succession of tenants who took little interest in the property, the village, or the church. There was plenty of scope for rich tenants who wished to enter into the life of the community.

When the firm became a public company in 1894, the only directors were

Arthur Liberty, William Street, and J. W. Howe. The staff of Liberty's registered relief that no outside director was to be appointed. Although they might chafe a bit at the paternalistic way the business was run, they liked the family feeling that prevailed. Mr Elsom was more amused by the Founder's irritability than upset; and George Ensworth's recollections of his 'sudden storms' were cancelled out by the consideration expressed when he was ill – 'Do not return until your Aunt deems it prudent'. Each new employee was chosen by Arthur Liberty himself, who looked for men and women capable of becoming experts in the merchandise of their departments. It was not regarded as nepotism but as natural that there were many Liberty, Blackmore, and Lasenby relatives in the firm. Many of the other staff also had family continuity, sons and daughters following fathers and mothers, many brothers, sisters, nephews, nieces, cousins. At one time, there were three sets of twins in the dressmaking workrooms.

The authorised capital of the Public Company was £200,000 in shares of £10 – which, according to Harmsworth's *Fortunes Made in Business* 'were eagerly taken up at a premium of 10s per £10 share'. The solicitors who handled the formation were Norton, Ross, Norton & Co. of Old Broad Street, with whom Harold Blackmore (the boy who wouldn't be kissed at the wedding) was articled. He was given the key of the Seal which matched Arthur Liberty's own, so that neither Mr Street nor Mr Howe could use the Seal except in the presence of either the Chairman or Blackmore. In 1900 he was given a seat on the Board to take charge of the legal work; and when Mr Howe retired in 1906 Blackmore was appointed Secretary. Two years later he gave up his practice to come in as a full time director. He was Chairman from 1936 until 1950. His son Hilary became a director of the firm in 1936; and Hilary's son, E. Anthony Blackmore, is a director now.

At the time of the formation of the public company, the *British Warehouseman* published an article entitled *The Liberty Art Movement*. Arthur Liberty was called 'The Man of the Moment in West End trade quarters, having recently converted his unique business into a limited liability company'. The uniqueness of the business lay in its having 'created an entirely new taste in fabrics, dress, and interior decoration, the word Liberty having become descriptive of the style . . . "I was determined," Mr Liberty said, "not to follow existing fashion but to create new ones."' His interviewer had been ushered into what he called the *sanctum sanctorum* after passing through a labyrinth of rooms in which 'the employment of electric light has developed a use for every turn and out-of-the-way corner one traverses, for each is utilised to display some rich or curious effect of oriental drapery and decoration'. He was invited to sit in a chair resembling a bishop's canopied throne, from which he observed a Sicilian Madonna enshrined above the chimneypiece, a Delft tiled mantel, an open box of Russian cigarettes on the desk, and a little dial of enamelled metal 'with a needle indicating whatever part of the house Mr Liberty desires to electrically communicate with' . . . surely the most splendid split infinitive in the history of journalism. During the interview, the Man of the Moment was asked if he had influenced Oscar Wilde, and he replied, 'Indeed, yes. My art fabrics were produced before he became a celebrity. I gave him his opportunity and he helped me mightily with mine through the publicity he commanded.' This was the year before the trial and imprisonment of Oscar Wilde, when 'the publicity he commanded' rebounded so mercilessly.

Two other appreciations written in the 1890s can be found, not of the Man of the Moment, but of the shop of the moment. In James Pope Hennessy's biography *Queen Mary*, the Crown Princess of Greece is writing a letter to her mother from London in July, 1896, when she was buying furniture for an English cottage she was building in the woods of Tatoi, above Athens: 'We spent I don't know how many hours at Maple and Liberty! I *screamed* at the things to Tino's horror, but they were too lovely! *No,* these shops I go mad in them! I would be ruined if I lived here longer! – Divine shops!!' The Crown Princess was as lavish with her exclamation marks as Queen Victoria. The second account is by Grace Lovat Fraser, American wife of the brilliant designer of sets and costumes for *The Beggar's Opera* and other stage productions. In 1898, when Grace was eight years old, she and her parents were staying at Morley's Hotel in Trafalgar Square. Writing seventy years later she recalled every detail of the beautiful clothes she was bought at Liberty's:

'I was treated to some fine new clothes, and for these we went to Liberty's. I shall never forget the lovely brown velvet coat trimmed with bands of beaver fur and the accompanying wide-brimmed velvet hat with soft feather pom-poms in pale gold and bronze. For afternoons there was a smocked dress of azure blue tussore silk embroidered with big white daisies, and for party occasions an ankle-length sheath of rose-pink brocade, patterned in two shades of deeper pink and lime green. The sleeves were long, tight medieval ones in lime-green silk embroidered all over with flowers in two shades of rose and deep green – a real aesthetic *fin de siècle* dress. These clothes took my breath away.' [1]

[1] *In the Days of My Youth* by Grace Lovat Fraser. Cassell, 1970.

9

ART NOUVEAU
JEWELLERY, SILVER, AND PEWTER

In the same year that Arthur Liberty left Farmer & Rogers to open his first half-shop, an art dealer of Hamburg named Samuel Bing visited the Far East and returned to Europe to open a gallery for Oriental Art in Paris, with a branch in New York. Twenty years later, in 1895, Bing opened a shop for modern art in the rue de Provence and called it L'ART NOUVEAU. It was this shop that gave a name to the new decorative style in France and England. The German term was *Jugendstil*, and in Italy it became known as *Stile Liberty*.

Four rooms in Bing's shop were designed by Henry van de Velde. Van de Velde became the best known of early Art Nouveau designers, but he was not the first. An earlier exponent was the American architect Louis Sullivan, who in 1880 designed the interior and furniture of the Auditorium Building in Chicago in what he himself called 'Quaint Style' – tangles of tendrils, scalloped leaves, and tortuous marine growths. In 1892 Victor Horta of Brussels began work on Professor Tassel's house at 6 rue Paul-Emile Janson, the interior decoration of which was inspired by the book illustrations of Aubrey Beardsley and Arthur Heygate Mackmurdo, founder of the Century Guild. Van de Velde began as a painter, but turned later to designing furniture, textiles, and metalwork, then eventually to architecture. He also acknowledged inspiration from Mackmurdo, and from English designers of the Arts and Crafts movement, in particular William Morris and Walter Crane – whose work he described as having '*les lignes de très spéciale souplesse*'. Furthermore, he paid tribute to Liberty silks, which he first saw in 1891 and described as bringing '*une sorte de printemps*' new to the Continental scene.

Indeed, it would be difficult to over-estimate the influence of British design on other countries towards the end of the century. English wallpapers were shown at *L'Exposition Universelle* of 1889 in Paris, and were afterwards imported into Belgium together with Liberty textiles and other 'artistic'

Art Nouveau side-board by Liberty & Co.

household furnishings from England, including pottery. Again, Liberty & Co. had a whole section in the Paris Exhibition of 1900. In René Schwaeblé's *Les Détraquées de Paris*, published at about this time, he writes of an apartment '*meublé luxueusement à l'anglaise*: modern style *chaises et fauteuils tortillés, tentures et tapis Liberty* etc.'.

In America, Louis Comfort Tiffany's work developed under the influence of the various English art and craft movements of the 1870s until he too arrived at Art Nouveau. Tiffany met Samuel Bing when he visited Paris for *L'Exposition Universelle* of 1889, and it was later at Bing's 'L'Art Nouveau' shop that the first pieces of iridescent Favrile glass designed by Tiffany were sold in Paris. Although his intention was to provide household objects whose beauty would enrich the lives of average American citizens, his glass was too elegant, exquisite, precious and impractical for everyday use. He and Morris had the same ideals and the same blind spots about the lives of 'average citizens' and what they could afford.

The world at large first became aware of the term Art Nouveau when van de Velde designed an Art Nouveau rest-room at the Dresden Art Exhibition of 1897. This rest-room, the decoration of which was as unrestful as a nightmare, so astonished and astounded that it became news beyond professional design circles. Three years later, the Paris Exhibition of 1900, at which Arthur Liberty was a juror, again brought the limelight on to what many people regarded as the Art Nouveau atrocities. In Vienna that same year, the work of 'The Glasgow Four' exhibited at the 8th Wiener Secessionist Exhibition made an international impact, and the same group received maximum attention when they exhibited again at the Turin Exhibition of 1902. The Glasgow School was led by Charles Rennie Mackintosh, architect of the controversial building for the Glasgow School of Art, his wife Margaret MacDonald, and Herbert and Frances McNair.

In wallpapers and furnishing textiles there was a great deal of distinguished designing. John Llewellyn was appointed to the Liberty Board in 1898, and it was under his inspired direction that Liberty's Art Nouveau furnishing fabrics were commissioned from many artists. It was Liberty's policy not to name their designers, but the Victoria & Albert Museum has confirmed that they included Lindsay P. Butterfield, C. F. A. Voysey, Frank Miles, Sidney Mawson, Arthur Willshaw, Edgar L. Pattison, J. M. Doran, Jessie M. King, and Arthur Wilcock. Wilcock in particular was much used by Liberty's in the 1890s; and his 'Daffodils and Crocus' chintz for them was bought by Walter Crane for his own diningroom. Liberty also had many designs from the Silver Studio, established by the designer craftsman Arthur Silver, who was chiefly inspired by Japanese examples. Hornsey College of Art now possesses the Silver Studio's Day Book for 1891–8, in which clients include Liberty, Morton, Richard Stanway and Lightbrown Aspinall; also sample books of designs, principally for wallpapers and cretonnes, but including designs for carpets and stencils for interior decoration. At Arthur Silver's early death in 1896, he left the Studio to be managed for his widow by Harry Napper, whose designs were also bought by Liberty. Subsequently Arthur's eldest son Rex directed the practice and, as will be told later, became an important designer of Liberty textiles, silver and pewter. His brother Harry Silver also designed textiles for Liberty's.

John Llewellyn was interviewed by *The Citizen* (December 10, 1898), on his appointment to the Board and he showed the journalist some new silk furnishing tapestry at 8s 9d a yard, 50 inches wide, saying that it could not have been bought ten years previously under 10 guineas a yard. It had only been perfected after many trials lasting over two years . . . 'These and other similar and characteristic patterns are now all the rage, not only in England but on the Continent, and indeed throughout the world. Just in the same way as there was a Louis XVI period, so we flatter ourselves that we have created a new "English" period. Years ago nothing but French designs would suit, now the English school is leading.' There would inevitably be imitators, not only at home but on the Continent – 'but this makes it necessary for us to have continual changes of patterns and fabrics in order to keep in front'.

Indeed there were imitators. In 1901 Liberty's were considerably gratified to be able to quote in translation a circular sent out by a firm of French silk manufacturers (not named) to their retail trade customers, upbraiding them for selling and advertising silks as being made in the *Style Liberty*:

'Gentlemen,

'We beg to draw your attention to the fact that by naming and describing our materials, manufactured in the new style, by the name of "Liberty" you gratuitously advertise – and without giving any credit to the French taste – a name which stands for nothing in regard to these creations, which are specialities due to inspiration purely French, and interpreted by French artists. The new style advances day by day, by reason of its undoubted merits; but this is due to the unremitting toil of French artists and manufacturers, and it is they who have the right to give the style a name. Their long years of effort, their self-sacrifice and perseverance, should attain other results than the glorification of the foreigner – or Liberty. Honour to whom honour is due; to the new style give the credit of its French good taste and originality; to the English give the credit of . . . such taste as they possess.'

The French successfully stamped out the use of the term *Style Liberty*, but in Italy *Stile Liberty* was applied to all Art Nouveau, not only in textiles, but in furniture, metalwork, glasswork, ceramics, and even architecture. And in Holland, the leading shop for modern furniture and furnishings, Metz & Co. of Amsterdam and The Hague began an association with Liberty & Co. which soon resulted in the name Liberty appearing in their advertising and, in the words of a Chairman of the firm, 'the second name of Metz rapidly became Liberty'. Seventy years later, Metz did in fact become Liberty, as will be told in the final chapter.

In furniture design, the Art Nouveau style gathered momentum until the exhibitions of 1900 in Paris and Vienna, and the Turin Exhibition of 1902. And as it gathered momentum, it also gathered excrescences. Although in the early years of the new century it was reasonably restrained in England, France and Belgium, in Germany and more particularly Austria perversions were rife. Furniture was produced with strange contortions and in asymmetrical shapes that affronted the senses. Surfaces were busily broken by panels of hammered copper, sometimes beaten with improving mottoes.

Pewter tea-set designed by Archibald Knox

British designers from whose work Continental Art Nouveau was originally derived, amongst them Walter Crane and C. R. Ashbee, reacted disgustedly against the distortions of the style. Lewis F. Day wrote in the *Art Journal* of October, 1900, that Art Nouveau 'shows symptoms . . . of pronounced disease'. And one of the most explosive outbursts was that of Arthur Liberty, after visiting an exhibition of Art Nouveau drawings and paintings in Budapest in 1909: 'It was painfully evident,' he wrote, 'that the very name *L'Art Nouveau* has been brought into contempt by gross exaggeration of its principles and aims. The majority of the exhibits were not only crude but meaningless. Nearly all the few clever ones were either obtrusively revolting in subject . . . or else erotic imaginings of morbid brains depicted with a mastery of technique only too wickedly perfect.' Arthur Liberty had been among the first to take an interest in Art Nouveau and experiment with the style when it promised to develop into a distinguished design movement. His reaction at its later manifestations was therefore all the more severe. There is a brief account of Liberty's introduction, development, and subsequent dismissal of Art Nouveau furniture and decoration written in the *Liberty Lamp* of July, 1927, by P. Campbell who worked in the Liberty cabinet factory from 1888:

'It was at this time that Mr Robinson and Mr Leonard Wyburd originated forms of modern design in interior work and furniture, which became known as "Art Nouveau", and I believe that the late Sir Arthur Liberty had hopes of founding a new School of Furniture of this type which would carry his name to posterity. For some years Art Nouveau was extremely popular, and we exhibited at the Arts and Crafts Exhibitions under the Presidency of Mr

Walter Crane and other well-known artists and designers. Gradually, however, the call for this decreased owing to the enormities carried out in its name on the Continent and especially Austria, and with the general public becoming more educated by such publications as *The Studio*, etc., a revulsion of feeling took place, and the demand came for period work such as Tudor, William and Mary, and the Brothers Adam.'

Another account of Liberty's changing styles in furniture was written by Guy Bentley: 'By the beginning of the 1890s, the characteristics of Liberty & Co. were slowly changing from the Eastern styles of furnishing; and for the past forty years [*he is writing in 1931*] the tendency has been to foster and develop our own natural styles of decoration, especially avoiding the French influence; in fact, French work has always been absent from our showrooms with the exception of one room in the style of Louis XVI, which was only a passing phase, acceding to the wish of one of the assistants who had a strong *penchant* for that period.

'During the last decade of the nineteenth century, the craving for something new at any cost produced the so-called Art Nouveau. This was never taken very seriously by the Furniture Department, and what little was done in it was carried out with considerable modifications. As we all know, it died a natural death and was unregretted, for in the form in which it developed on the Continent, especially, it passed all bounds of reason. A good deal of work was done in an attempted revival of ancient Celtic, and I have always regretted that it failed to find more lasting favour, being one of the most brilliant phases of art that ever existed. Moreover, it was indigenous and British, with little or no debt to foreign influence. The "Book of Kells" showed it at its highest development, fully justifying the saying that it is "the wonder and despair" of copyists; but when simplified it does not lose its individuality. The finials of the staircase at Chesham House were a highly successful modern adaptation.'

The Celtic revival began with the finding of the Tara brooch in 1850 which inspired silversmiths and book illustrators. Copies of antique Irish ornaments were shown by James West & Sons of Dublin at the 1851 Exhibition and also by Waterhouse of Dublin. Both firms showed

Celtic finial, Chesham House

more jewellery of Celtic Irish inspiration at the Exhibition of Art Industry in Dublin in 1853. Morris, Faulkner & Co. made a cabinet in 1861 of inlay work with Celtic-inspired initials on the lid, and Celtic designs with the interlac motif began to appear in magazines and pattern books. Christopher Dresser wrote of Celtic ornaments in his *Modern Ornamentation* published in 1886; and the Glasgow School expressed the indigenous Celtic principles with coils and linear rhythms, interlac, and the dragon or serpent motifs kept on one plane raised above the background. In 1899 Liberty & Co. launched their Cymric silver. Stephan Tschudi Madsen, in his *Sources of Art Nouveau*, writes of 'the ever-vigilant Arthur Liberty's' Cymric silver and Tudric pewter being 'the last important result of the neo-Celtic tendency, an expression of the formal fusion of the stylistic elements of Art Nouveau and the Celtic'. Madsen went on to say that the influence of the Celtic revival on Art Nouveau was confined to Scandinavia, Scotland and Ireland, with a few special fields in England, mainly silverwork and book illustration . . . 'Only in Norway and Sweden was the influence of any importance to furniture making, interior design, or architecture.' We can but regret with Guy Bentley that Liberty's were unable to gain for it more lasting favour in those fields.

However, their beautiful Cymric silver and Tudric pewter of Celtic inspiration were among the most distinguished contributions to this felicitous development of Art Nouveau. It was sold in the Jewellery Department, which was first started in 1883 and originally concentrated on Eastern silverware and bijouterie, Cairene and Indian work in gold and precious stones. Later, notable specialities were jade and amber. Besides rare and costly antique jewellery, the department carried quite inexpensive pieces, described in one contemporary editorial as 'unique and dainty ornaments in gold and silver, quaint conceits and devices from China and Japan' . . . forerunners of 'costume jewellery', although of course the gold and silver were real. They concentrated on Eastern work because it was in keeping with the traditions of the firm, and also because at that time European jewellery and silverware design was contemptible. The long Napoleonic wars which halted the interchange of craftsmanship in Europe began the decline; and then the rapid development of machine industry brought about virtual stagnation in design. Bentley wrote of the jewellery and silverware illustrated in the catalogue of the Great Exhibition of 1851 that 'there was scarcely a specimen which could be called even creditable in design, and many of them are veritable nightmares'. He went on: 'This Exhibition opened the eyes of people of good natural taste; and the schools of design which were established soon after, together with the interest already aroused by the Gothic revival, began to stir the dry bones, and by slow degrees an improvement became general. William Morris and the Hardmans of Birmingham contributed to this improvement during the 60s and 70s.'

To supplement their Eastern imports, Liberty began to import Dutch and Greek silver jewellery; and then they founded their own workshops, at first making reproductions of Flemish and Renaissance pieces, and then developing their own Liberty tradition alongside the Eastern imports. In 1899 came the great impetus given by 'Liberty Cymric'. Bernard Cuzner, Jessie M. King and Rex Silver designed the first Cymric jewellery which, enriched with blue and green enamels, was instantly successful. In 1901 a new company, Liberty & Co. (Cymric) Ltd was registered in conjunction with the old Birmingham firm of W. H. Haseler. Guy Bentley emphasises that 'from the first the silver plate was kept sternly to restrained and refined elegance, natural forms of flowers and foliage being always excluded as well as the Rococo and shell ornament of the previous fashions. Then a new decorative artist, Archibald Knox, brought out a series of designs for the Cymric Silver Company based more or less on ancient Celtic art – cups, vases, inkstands, and other silver articles, sometimes combining old and precious stones. It was soon realised that the Celtic forms were equally suited for pewter, and the manufacture of Tudric pewter began in 1903'. There is reason to believe that some designs were in production as early as 1901.

The pewter trade had been virtually extinct in England since the mid-nineteenth century . . . killed by the introduction of Britannia metal and electro-plating, the general deterioration of taste, and the cheap production of domestic earthenware, pottery, and porcelain. A revival began towards the end of the nineteenth century in Germany, the exponents of Art Nouveau seeing in pewter a medium after their own hearts. German *Jugendstil* in pewter developed in a more controlled manner than in other fields. In a paper on pewter read in 1904 before the Applied Art Section of the Society of Arts, Arthur Liberty observed, 'Alongside the foolish and undesirable, it must in justice be admitted that the Germans have recently produced many original and pleasing designs in pewter.'

The German firm of J. P. Kayser Sohn of Krefeld, founded in 1885, exhibited their Kayserzinn pewter at the Paris *Exposition Universelle* of 1900; and from that time until 1914 it was stocked by Liberty. The first Liberty catalogue introducing '*Novelties in Pewter Ware*' (1900) included a claret jug by Walter Scherf & Co. of Nuremburg – a tall jug whose design was typical of the Art Nouveau manner, with grapes and leaves clustered at the top, the stems trailing diagonally downwards to the base. This jug was stocked by Liberty for many years. The majority of the illustrations accompanying Arthur Liberty's paper on pewter when it was printed in the

Journal of the Society of Arts, June 10, 1904, were of Liberty Tudric. It was priced, he said, to bring it within the reach of people of moderate means, and was not identical in its constituents to the old material. It comprised some ingredients to make it more brilliant in appearance and harder in texture. And it was of uniform quality, whereas antique pewter varies greatly.

The two most important designers for Liberty & Co. (Cymric) Ltd were Rex Silver and the Manx artist Archibald Knox, who began to supply designs to Liberty in the 1890s. As with so many English designers (including those from whom Continental designers had originally drawn their inspiration for Art Nouveau) Knox was hostile to the swirling excesses of the style as it developed on the Continent. His own work, although it had a feeling of growth and freedom, derived rather from the disciplined interlacing of Celtic ornamentation found on Manx and Cornish crosses and in illuminated manuscripts. He therefore fell in very happily with Arthur Liberty's own suggestion that the new pewter ware should be decorated with modifications of ancient Celtic forms supplemented by floral and plant motifs used in a controlled and stylised manner. Liberty's policy that their designers should be anonymous makes definite identification seldom possible. But Knox's style was so distinctive that V. & A. experts can attribute his work with some degree of certainty. According to Guy Bentley, Knox did over four hundred designs for Liberty's, the majority being for their Cymric silver and jewellery. A whole series was based on ancient Celtic art and the same designs were produced in a range of Tudric pewter which, Guy Bentley recorded, 'produced something of a furore'.

Celtic forms were also used in the decoration of a splendid range of Liberty garden pottery made by Mrs G. F. Watts, widow of the painter, who had her own pottery at Compton. Her work for Liberty won Gold and Silver Medal awards from the Royal Botanic Society and Royal Horticultural Society. The pottery was in 'frost proof earthenware, red or grey, that with exposure assumes an interesting old-world and weather stained appearance'. It included shrub pots, flower pots, bird baths, window boxes, garden seats and benches, pedestals, sundials, fountains and terrace balustrades. Mrs Watts also designed carpets and rugs made in Donegal for Liberty's. It was a unique concession that Liberty's should have credited the designer's name. Mrs Watts was evidently a woman who got her own way. Archibald Knox also designed Donegal rugs and carpets for Liberty's – but anonymously.

10

THE BELLE EPOQUE – IN LONDON
AND AT THE LEE

For fashionable Society in London and Paris, the Edwardian period was the Belle Epoque. It was a period of unparalleled expenditure on extravagant pleasures and elaborate fashions, a golden age for those who had the gold. In commerce, everything was basking in what seemed to be perpetual prosperity. And the great department stores of London were at their zenith.

It was high noon also for the English country-house way of life. And Arthur Liberty had the best of both worlds, the golden commerce and the golden countryside. After he had been ten years a tenant of Lee Manor, the Plaistowes sold the property to Arthur Vernon, an auctioneer of High Wycombe related to the Libertys; and in 1902 he sold it to Arthur Liberty. From then on he gradually added to the manor house, and acquired more land until he owned 3,000 acres, also farms, cottages, houses, and the Lee Gate Inn. He gave the village a green, planted woods and avenues of trees, and had a new road made across his fields to Great Missenden station because he considered the existing road too hilly for his horses. There was a locked gate at each end of the new road, to which only the Liberty family had keys. He had a studio and office at the Manor, but still went up by train to London most weekdays. At Marylebone station he had a marble seat built for himself alone to repose upon if he arrived early for his homeward train. Every summer there was a day on which the whole staff of Liberty & Co., with their families, were transported to The Lee Manor, where there was luncheon and tea in a great marquee on the lawn.

He was gradually giving more of his time and energy to being a country squire, less to being a retailer of Regent Street. He became chairman of many county associations, among them the Bucks Architectural and Archaeological Society, and the Bucks Association for the Loan of Pictures to Schools. He became High Sheriff of the County, a Justice of Peace, Chairman of the Great Missenden Petty Sessions, a County Councillor, Deputy Lieutenant of the County. He initiated the building of two new transepts to

The Lee Manor from across the village green

Drawing-room at The Lee Manor. Note the bronze stork

the church, an extension of the nave, a baptistry and new vestry, and a heating system. He engaged C. H. Fellowes Prynne as architect, and himself provided all but £550 of the total cost. He founded and edited The Lee Parish Magazine, allowing each of the three non-conformist chapels in the village a page in which to publish whatever they wished – a unique ecumenical gesture at that time; he included children of all denominations at the annual Sunday School fête he gave in the Manor grounds, and every Good Friday they were invited to receive a hot cross bun from the Lady of the Manor on the terrace outside the drawing room. Emma Louise was very happy with her garden, her role as Lady Bountiful, and her work on the Board of Management of the Royal Bucks Hospital, Aylesbury. Both she and Arthur were very fond of children, and filled the Manor with nephews and nieces on long visits. Mary and Phyllis Stewart spent much of their girlhood at the Manor. Mary (now Mrs Cummins and still living in The Lee village) remembers her uncle as 'very kind and accessible, very generous'. Generous indeed – one Christmas morning the two sisters each found a £1,000 note under their breakfast plates.

Each summer there was The Lee Week, during which cricket matches were played (mixed, men and girls) against teams got up by neighbouring Buckinghamshire families. There was a tennis tournament, and dancing every night. A favourite game was the Night Attack, when acetylene lamps were placed at intervals round the Manor. The attack was by a 'Missenden Army', the house-party forming the defenders. The Squire was at Sundial Corner, Mrs Liberty guarded the front door; Aunt Eliza was placed at the pond, Phyllis and Mary Stewart at the summerhouse, and so on. The Missenden Army blew a hooter at 9.30 p.m., the Manor dinner-gong replied, a rocket was sent up and a shot rang out. The attackers crept up in the dark by devious routes and attempted to get through the defenders without being touched. Attackers and defenders

THE ODD UNCLE ARTHUR

Caricature by Jack Hassall in *Ye Lee Week*, record of the Cricket Week matches and jollities

Bronze stork 'suitable for Halls, Conservatories, Libraries, etc.'. Curio catalogue, *c.* 1890

eventually repaired to the Manor for a splendid supper. Uncle Arthur's own favourite game was billiards, which the family encouraged as they thought it good for his figure.

In spite of his delights and fulfilments as Squire, he was still very much involved with London commitments. One of these was the revival of the British silk industry which had declined ever since Cobden's treaty with France in 1860 when the import duty on silk was repealed. By the 1880s, a decade of general trade depression, the industry was in dire straits. Arthur Liberty instituted an improved school of design, and in 1888 held an exhibition at East India House, at which a loom was set up with a Spitalfields weaver at work. Three years later, the Silk Association of Great Britain and Ireland was formed, with Sir Thomas Wardle as President and Arthur Liberty as Vice-President. A little book on the history of silk fabrics entitled *Sericulture,* written by Guy Bentley, was published by Liberty & Co.; and a British Silk Renaissance Exhibition was held at Chesham House. There was a dazzling list of patrons, headed by Her Royal Highness the Princess Mary Adelaide, Duchess of Teck, and including two other Duchesses, seventeen Countesses, two Viscountesses, sixteen Ladies, and only one plain Mrs. It also included some influential Knights, Walter Crane, and a whole clutch of RAS and ARAS.

It was in this year that John Llewellyn became head of Liberty's silk department. Under his inspired direction many new fabrics were developed in co-operation with British manufacturers. In an interview with *The Citizen* on his appointment to the Board in 1898, he describes some of the most recent introductions. They included a softly draping 'Liberty Gareze', various new silks and velvets, and an entirely new dress fabric named Orion satin. He explained that the aim had been to get a wide-width satin of the same brilliancy as the most expensive Italian satins. It should be at once crisp and elastic, should not crease, and at the same time should ensure perfectly graceful draping . . . 'Orion satin,' said Llewellyn, 'may be run through the hand or put through a ring and will not leave behind the slightest crease.' The interviewer asked him where the designs for printed fabrics came from, and he replied : 'It is of no matter to us where a design comes from so long as it possesses merits worthy to be put before the public by the House of Liberty. We collect designs from all quarters.'

There is a possibility that some time in the Edwardian period Liberty's bought some designs from D. H. Lawrence. In *Sons & Lovers*, published in 1913 and believed to be largely autobiographical, Paul Morel spreads out before Miriam some brownish linen with a design of roses stencilled on it. She asks him what he will do with it, and he replies 'Send it to Liberty's'. Later she reminds him to bring her 'that letter from the man at Liberty's'; and in Chapter 12 we find, 'He was gradually making it possible to earn a livelihood by his art. Liberty's had taken several of his painted designs on various stuffs, and he could sell designs for embroideries for altar-cloths, and similar things, in one or two places.'

For the Coronation of King Edward VII, there was a royal command that the robes of peeresses and all Court dresses be made entirely in British silk. The Silk Association held an exhibition at the Hanover Gallery the previous February. Once more there was a glittering list of titled patrons, headed this time by the Princess of Wales, herself President of the Ladies' National Silk Association. Among the more fulsome press reports was that of *Black and White* eulogising on 'the superb beauty of the brocades and crepes, figured silks and printed gauzes that England's workers, under the direction of the great Liberty firm, have produced. We prate about the fabrics and intelligent manufacturers of France, whilst here in our own land has arisen the king of all silk manufacture, the manufacturer who has touched the highest possible point in the modern making of silks, and who is as well the leading colourist of the loveliest fabrics to be found in Europe'. They were wrong in calling him a manufacturer, but right in saying the silks were produced 'under the direction of the great Liberty firm'.

The fashions of the Belle Epoque were very different from the aesthetic attire for which Liberty had become celebrated; and the titled ladies who condescended so charmingly at the silk exhibitions were very different from the aesthetic guests at Grosvenor Gallery private views. Gone, quite gone, were the marble-pale, melancholy faces under the fringe of auburn hair; gone, quite gone, the languid droop. Backbones and fine bosoms were back, with tight-laced hand-span waists; and the Edwardian

Belle Epoque hat by Liberty, trimmed ostrich feather

beauties, whether of Stage or Society, were all smiles and dimples. They went
in for flirtatious raillery, not intense communication with kindred souls. The
most admired women were those of 'a certain age' and of an implied but not
specified experience. And the favoured artists were the fashionable portrait
painters: Sargent, de Laszlo, Lavery, Boldini. Nevertheless, Liberty's continued to design and make aesthetic dresses based on classical lines. Their
catalogues were divided into two sections. The first was entitled *Costumes
Never out of Fashion*, illustrating the high-waisted, classically draped gowns of
the Empire; the second section was entitled *Novelties for the New Season*,
clothes based on the prevailing fashion stemming from the couture houses of
Paris. These were all model gowns, to be ordered made-to-measure. Other
catalogues held many of the things in which the Edwardian lady delighted.
For example, *Chiffoneries and Fantasies* illustrated the elaborate blouses that
were the sublimation of Edwardiana, all tucks and frills and cascading tor-
rents of lace. These blouses, pouched over the tiny belted-in waist, made a
shrine of the mysterious one-piece bosom. Jewellery catalogues have pages
of silver clasps for the petersham belts which held together the elaborate
blouse and the sweeping skirt; also the monstrous hat-pins, that were
plunged into the monumental hats on which flowers, bird's wings – even
complete birds – were mounted. The jewellery department was a market for
the world's most tempting fairings: Norwegian enamel-work and silver-
gilt 'specially and exclusively produced for Liberty & Co.'; Dutch wrought-
silver jewellery, Indian silver bangles, Chinese wrought-silver brooches,
Japanese silver sleeve links, Damascus single-twist bangles, gold Etruscan
brooches.

Liberty's reputation for jewellery had become international, even to
reaching foreign courts. When Kaiser Wilhelm II was at Buckingham
Palace as the guest of George v for the ceremonial unveiling of the Victoria
Memorial in 1911, he commanded that a selection of Indian jewellery be
brought for his inspection. A. W. Foster recalled taking it:

'I arrived soon after 9 a.m., but he was extremely busy, so much so that it was
nearly 2 o'clock before I got my chance. In the meantime, a kindly official
took me down to the Buttery, where I was refreshed with the strongest pre-
war whisky and soda I have ever experienced. When finally the jewellery was
chosen, I accompanied one of the Kaiser's bodyguards, a towering German
cavalryman with glittering helmet, well over six foot in height, to the
Grosvenor Hotel, where part of his suite was lodged, and there received the
money. I shall not forget his contemptuous air whilst we were together – I
suppose it was typical.'

LIBERTY & CO LTD

DESIGNERS AND MAKERS OF
FURNITURE
CARPETS ARTISTIC FABRICS WARES
DRESSES AND JEWELRY

TO THE KING

TO THE QUEEN

BY APPOINTMENT

■ TELEGRAMS ■
LIBERTEZ LONDON

REGENT STREET LONDON
AVENUE DE L'OPERA PARIS

■ BANKERS ■
BANK OF ENGLAND

Letter heading at the time of the Belle Epoque

Liberty & Co. were granted many Royal Warrants: East Indian Merchants and Manufacturers of Art Fabrics to Queen Victoria; Manufacturers of Art Fabrics to King Edward VII; Gold and Silversmiths to Queen Alexandra; Manufacturers of Art Fabrics to King George V; and Silk Mercers to Queen Mary. A member of the staff remembered when, a Royal Warrant having been granted, he was sent to fetch it from the house of the Lord Chamberlain. 'I was confronted by the butler who said, "Oh, yes, it has been granted to your people, but until the Lord Chamberlain has signed it, you can't have it, and it depends upon when I put it before His Lordship as to when you will get it." However, he didn't get the expected tip; a few words with the Lord Chamberlain by one of our Directors soon put the matter right.'

The Belle Epoque ended with the death of the pleasure-loving King. In fashion, the chic silhouette had already begun to alter. In the autumn of 1906, the wife of Paul Poiret, the rising young dress designer, had appeared in a clinging gown without corset. It was the first straw in the wind of change – or one might say the first whale-bone to be cast to the wind. From then on Poiret influenced more and more elegant women to unshackle their bodies. In May 1908, *Vogue* was reporting: 'The fashionable figure is growing straighter and straighter, less bust, less hips, more waist, and a wonderfully long, slender suppleness about the limbs . . . the long skirt reveals plainly every line and curve of the leg from hip to ankle. The leg has suddenly become fashionable.' And Isadora Duncan 'for the first time visited a fashionable dressmaker and fell to the fatal lure of stuffs, colours, form. I, who had always worn a little white tunic, succumbed to the enticement of ordering and wearing beautiful gowns'. [1] The fact that she was currently the mistress of a millionaire may have had something to do with it, but her account goes on, 'Only I had one excuse, the dressmaker was no ordinary one, but a genius – Paul Poiret, who could dress a woman in such a way as to create a work of art. Yet this was for me the change from sacred to profane art.'

[1] *My Life* by Isadora Duncan. Gollancz, 1928.

In 1909 Diaghilev's Russian Ballet burst upon Paris with what many may have thought was profane art . . . the pulsating colours, orgiastic sensuality, frenetic leaps and savage rhythms. Léon Bakst's costumes brought into vogue a new oriental look with harem skirts, turbans, heavy gold chains, bangles and bracelets. It was a look that Poiret, who had always to be first, claimed he had already launched. The Orient of Diaghilev, Bakst, and Poiret was not the Orient of the aesthetes. The fabrics were not the soft silks in pastel tints that Liberty imported. As Osbert Lancaster put it in *Homes Sweet Homes*, 'Before one could say Nijinsky the pale pastel shades which had reigned supreme on the walls of Mayfair for almost two decades were replaced by a riot of barbaric hues – jade green, purple, every variety of crimson and scarlet, and, above all, orange.'

With its Paris branch taking the feverish temperature, Liberty's revised their colours. An editorial in *The Queen* in 1910 describing a Poiret collection shows that he was obtaining some of his fabrics from Liberty – and possibly some of his ideas as well:

'This season there is evidently a general leaning towards the Oriental, which expresses itself definitely in turbans and Indian cachemires. Every mannequin had her pretty head enveloped in a coloured silk handkerchief, twisted like a turban, and in a shade to go with her gown. One very pretty girl had on a pink mauve turban and a gown in which the lower half of the skirt was in old rose Liberty, and the upper half in mauve *mousseline de soie*, slightly gathered both in the high waist and the knees. The corsage was pure Madame Récamier style.'

Well, of course, pure Récamier high-waisted Empire style had been a Liberty constant ever since the opening of the Costume Department. It is interesting that the writer, although an Englishwoman, used the word Liberty in a generic sense, as did the French. A *Daily Chronicle* Paris correspondent at about this time reported: 'Mr Lasenby Liberty has given a new word to the French language, which is something for an Englishman to have done, is it not? It was Paris and the Parisians who first discovered the magic of his British-manufactured silks and dropped the word "soie" for "Liberty"; the latter word alone is all-sufficing.' And in Nice, Isadora Duncan's millionaire invited a large party to be his guests at a carnival ball at the Casino, 'providing pierrot costumes for everyone, made in flowing Liberty satin'. Pierrot costumes could hardly be more divergent from the Hellenic lines that Isadora usually affected; but perhaps the flowing Liberty satin rendered the costumes more aesthetic than Pierrot ever was. Isadora's life-long devotion to Liberty's permits one to speculate whether it was a devotion even unto death – whether the long scarf which strangled her in that tragic motor accident on the Riviera in 1927 can have been a Liberty scarf.

The Russian Ballet did not come to London until 1911, but Paul Poiret arrived with his collection in 1909 at the invitation of Mrs Asquith, wife of the Prime Minister. Margot Asquith had seen *Schéhérazade* in Paris, had visited Poiret's couture house, and had declared his collection simply must be shown in London. She would arrange for this to be at No. 10 Downing Street. It was a time of crisis for British textile and clothing interests, and tariff reform was under debate. Questions about the Poiret fashion show were asked in the House, and it is on record that 160 newspapers and magazines expressed outrage at the Prime Minister's wife using No. 10 Downing Street (Gowning Street, of course, in the popular press) for a display of foreign fashions. Typical of press reaction was the *Nottingham Daily Express*: 'The spectacle of the wife of the English Prime Minister posing as the advertising agent for a Parisian dressmaker is not a pleasing one. It is the height of indiscretion!'

But indiscretion was one of Margot Asquith's most endearing characteristics, and everyone knew and accepted that the discretion of his wife was something quite outside the power of the Prime Minister to control. She hastened, of course, to order a whole host of new dresses from London houses, and the affair ended with a brilliantly diplomatic letter from Poiret to the press in which he stressed the internationality of fashion. Many of his dresses, he said, were made of Liberty fabrics. He had bought a Burberry travelling coat and ordered several suits from Poole's. Insularity was ungrateful, after all 'it is quite possible that M. Clemenceau himself dresses in London ... anything English is fashionable in France'.

Mr Asquith soon had other woman trouble besides that caused by his wife. The Suffragettes organised an attack upon the West End shops for March 1st, 1912. At 4 o'clock, almost every shop window from Piccadilly Circus up the length of Regent Street and along much of Oxford Street, was broken by women striking them with hammers they had concealed in their muffs or other parts of their dress. Liberty's was one of the shops to suffer, and an 'artist's impression' showing the elegant arched windows of East India House with the name LIBERTY & CO above them, appeared with astounding speed in the *Daily Graphic* the following morning, over the caption 'Disgraceful Scenes in the West End – Wholesale Window Smashing by Suffragettes'.

On Monday March 4, *The Standard* published some of the reader's letters they had received about the affair, top position being given to one from Mr Lasenby Liberty:

'As the vicarious victim of the recent raid it would be deemed an act of grace if Mrs Pankhurst, on behalf of her fair legions, would state the mental process by which they deem the breaking of the very shrines at which they worship will advance their cause.'

Mr Liberty did not know his Mrs Pankhurst if he really believed that she worshipped at the shrine of fashion – although the Suffragettes were always careful to dress well enough to avoid any suggestion of 'unwomanliness'. Another letter to *The Standard* came from Mrs Lily Watson of Streatham Hill, a member of a county education authority, who wrote protesting against 'the disgraceful acts of lawlessness and outrage perpetrated in the name of the woman's cause . . . I can hardly imagine any lady, of whatever political party she may be, who does not feel the utmost disgust on reading in Saturday's paper of the public degradation of womanhood. Words fail me, and I am oddly reminded of the time-honoured saying in *Punch*: "It's worse than wicked; it's vulgar"'.

More than two hundred women were arrested (for damage to property, not vulgarity). They were mostly students, nurses and artists, but those sent to prison included the distinguished musician Dr (later Dame) Ethel Smythe. In the following year Robinson & Cleaver, Swan & Edgar, Swears & Wells, the White House Linen Specialists, and T. J. Harries sued the officials of the Women's Social & Political Union for the damage to their windows. They won their case, and were awarded £364. Mr Liberty was not amongst the plaintiffs. He probably considered it ungentlemanly to bring an action against ladies, however unladylike their behaviour.

Mr and Mrs Liberty in Granada, 1910, recalling the fashion for 'Moorish schemes' in the early days of Liberty's Furnishing and Decoration Studio

II

MERCHANT ADVENTURING
OVERSEAS CONTRACTS; WORLD WAR I

The Chairman could well afford to be magnanimous about the damage to his windows. The financial position was rosy, the future stretched ahead full of bright promise. The *London Evening News* wrote of his annual report in February, 1912: 'Liberty's can pride themselves upon presenting the soundest balance-sheet in the world of dress. The Ordinary dividend of 20 per cent has been steadily maintained for years. The capital of the company is practically represented by the freehold and leasehold properties and goodwill. The Preference shares are more than covered by investments, and the reserve funds today amount to £321,000. These extraordinary results are due to the chairman, Mr Arthur Lasenby Liberty, whose genius for finance is only equalled by his excellent taste and sound business qualities.'

To which could be added a talent for merchant adventuring. A Harmsworth publication *Fortunes Made in Business* (Part 5, 1900) had an article referring in poetic strain to people working for Liberty's all over the oriental world ... 'Quaint parchment-skinned pedlars are wandering throughout the length and breadth of China gathering together ancient embroideries of wonderful colourings, and throughout Persia and among the temples of India the same thing is going on. Dark-eyed women are always at work in Smyrna and Bokhara, slowly threading fine materials for sale in Regent Street. Thousands of rare and ancient curios find their way by devious channels to the same busy mart, and so do prayer rugs (worn by the knees of the faithful) from all corners of the Moslem world.' It was not only quaint parchment-skinned pedlars who were wandering around the Orient for Liberty's; white-skinned department buyers (no doubt wearing three-piece business suits) were sent on long voyages of exploration. For example Mr King, who became head of the Carpet Department in 1905, made several journeys to the Near East. Guy Bentley described his knowledge of oriental carpets as 'extensive and peculiar'. But all Liberty buyers, if not peculiar, had extensive knowledge of their speciality.

93

PROTECTIVE MIMICRY.

Artful the Chameleon (on Young Turkey Carpet). "I THOUGHT I COULD MANAGE SOMEHOW TO TAKE THE COLOUR OF MY SURROUNDINGS, BUT I'M NOT AT ALL SURE THAT THESE LIBERTY DESIGNS WON'T BE TOO MUCH FOR ME."

By Lindley Sambourne; *Punch*, April 28, 1909

Arthur Liberty himself made many voyages – holidays in one sense, but always on the look out for unusual merchandise. He kept journals on these travels, and several were published: *The Treasure Hunt*; *Springtime in the Basque Mountains*; *Pictorial Records of Japan* (photographs by Mrs Liberty), *A Day in Tangier*. Others were bound in typescript for the family and friends. One expedition to Constantinople was purely for business, and proved an unnecessary journey. It was in 1909, soon after the Young Turk Revolution. Liberty's received a message that there were treasures in the Sultan's Palace that might be acquired at bargain prices. The Chairman and one of his managers set out forthwith. They were received at the Porte by a Prince of the Royal blood. A day or two afterwards they were taken to Yildiz Kiosk, imagining they were going to inspect the treasures and take their pick. On arrival there, however, they were charged a franc for admission to the Palace, which had become a public museum. It made a good anecdote for Arthur Liberty to recount at dinner parties, and he used to say, 'It was the charming oriental way of informing us we had been humbugged.'

The outbreak of war put an end to merchant adventuring. One of the last exhibitions held at Chesham House was of ancient prayer-rugs from Eastern palaces. It was described in the *Building News* of May 15, 1914: 'Among the exhibits there is a pilgrim rug dating from the 16th century. It has the green niche, recognised as a proof that it has been at Mecca. So rare are these specimens that only five or six may be gathered in a period of many years' collecting. Two dozen other valuable prayer-rugs are displayed, brought from the Holy Land round Smyrna and Ephesus. There is a Persian palace carpet 22 ft by 9 ft 4 in., in fine preservation; also Mosque carpets and rugs from the Caucasus mountains as fine as silk; some specimens from Khorassan, silk rugs from Bokhara, almost blood red; from Herat a rug 200 years old, woven in old Persian colours; Chinese rugs of exquisite design in flame, rich blue of the Celestial Empire, and Imperial yellow.'

In furniture, this pre-war period suffered a general reaction from Art Nouveau – everyone was playing safe. People bought late eighteenth-century furniture, genuine and reproduction. Japanese and Chinese furniture was also very popular for Edwardian drawing-rooms and bedrooms, with bamboo furniture for conservatories and the 'Winter Gardens' of hotels. In fact, everybody was doing what Liberty had done on their own thirty years previously – but Liberty's own cabinet factories were now producing what Guy Bentley described as 'furniture and fittings of sound workmanship and style of the best period of "English Domestic" – not spurious modern antiques, mere copies of examples of past times, but taking inspiration from them, and producing woodwork in the spirit of old work which lasts for generations'.

Bentley also refers to a passing vogue for painted furniture:

'A curious fashion prevailed during some years of this period, which is now almost forgotten, viz. furniture made of light coloured wood (pine or ash), stained in a fancy colour – green, blue, terracotta, red and even crimson. Purists – and I among them – always protested against imparting to wood a colour which it never had or could have naturally, thereby differing essentially from stain, which only imparts the appearance of age. Paint and enamel, not only in white and cream, but in various other tints, were also in vogue for furniture, especially bedroom suites.'

This particular outbreak of coloured furniture was started by Paul Poiret in 1912 with his Martine furniture designed by Pierre Fauconnet. It was at about this time that Poiret set up a London branch of his Martine decorating business in Albemarle Street, appointing as manager Marcel Boulestin – later more successfully a restaurant proprietor. The Duchesse de Gramont summed up the Martine stained furniture as 'a night of bad dreams after

eating potted hare'. Some even more indigestible painted furniture was produced by the Omega Workshops, started in 1913 under the inspiration and
direction of Roger Fry, painter, art critic and historian, with backing from
William Foxton. Omega productions included textiles of cubist character, a
few dress fashions, some pottery, and what John Gloag describes as 'plain,
ill-constructed furniture covered with vivid painted patterns. The designers
of this furniture were wholly preoccupied with colour and indifferent to and
apparently ignorant of structural common sense. This was an artistic experiment that contributed nothing to the development of furniture design.' [1]

In contrast, the Continent was in a fever of design activity. The catalyst
had been the Ballets Russe in 1909. The previous year the Munich Exhibition of Applied Art had begun disseminating a decisive influence on decoration. The formalised floral motifs in vivid but flat colourings, and the use of
black backgrounds, were fore-runners of the style that eventually became
known in the mid-1960s as Art Deco. In 1911 there was the first Cubist
exhibition, which spread Cubism beyond the circle of Picasso and Braque. In
Italy the Futurists were beginning to be seriously discussed. And in Munich,
Kandinsky and Franz Marc founded the Blaue Reiter (Blue Horseman)
group. Marc was killed at Verdun, but Kandinsky survived to become a
Bauhaus teacher. In 1911 Poiret started his Atelier Martine of very young
students, and it was seen as the start of a new art movement, blending primitive naïveté with ultra-modern sophistication.

Meanwhile Liberty's Contracts Department was being kept busy decorating new hotels and re-decorating old ones. Previously, ladies never dined
out in restaurants; but it now became immensely fashionable to dine at the
Savoy Hotel (nowhere else) on Sunday nights – Sunday because there was
the excuse that it enabled one's own servants to go to Evensong. Another
aspect of the Edwardian way of social life was the Friday to Monday week-
end house-party. Many owners of country houses became conscious of their
spartan bedrooms, worn carpets, mildewed curtains, and insufficient near-
primitive bathrooms. To all of this, Liberty were equipped to attend. A
member of the Contracts staff later recalled this Edwardian hey-day:

'In 1898 the Cabinet Factories had moved from Newman Yard to Dufours
Place, Soho, from where we carried out large orders and contracts, such as
Wadhurst Park, the Piccadilly Hotel, etc. Then in 1912 we moved to
Highgate. This was a complete up-to-date factory, and for the first time we
had machinery and stocks of timber which might be regarded as worthy and

[1] *A Short Dictionary of Furniture* by John Gloag. George Allen & Unwin, revised
edition, 1969.

adequate to the far larger and higher class of business which became entrusted to our hands. And with the advent of the genial and ever-ready Mr "Bert" Pannell at the head of affairs, a new era commenced. From Highgate we turned out first-class work, and produced all over the United Kingdom and abroad various types of interior fitments and decoration which I am confident will in time to come be looked upon, and spoken of, as masterpieces of design and craftsmanship.'

Linen-fold panelling was a Liberty speciality for halls, libraries, galleries, corridors, billiard rooms. The elegant plasterwork of ceilings and cornices was more classic than rococo. Entrance halls were made impressive with massive doorways, archways, carved chimney pieces, deep window-sills. The Liberty style at this time might be called Abbotsford Baronial – less oppressive than Balmoral Baronial and without the stags' heads and tartan. It was Guy Bentley who directed most of the work, and he is remembered as a man of great elegance, who always carried a furled umbrella. When measuring doorways, embrasures, or windows, he would use his umbrella as a measure, directing his assistant to write down: 'Height four umbrellas; width two umbrellas plus two ferrules', and so on.

European contracts included large orders in Rotterdam, Alsace, Venice, Monaco, Genoa, Budapest: and it was said that Liberty at this time did work of one sort or another for nearly all the *haute noblesse* of France. Further afield, there were many decorating contracts for Indian Rajahs and Princes. In South Africa, one particularly large contract at Wynber was supervised by Mr Wolfe (The Old Grey Wolfe), who during his service with the company travelled 47,000 miles. In the summer of 1914, his colleague Mr Butler was learning Russian before going out to supervise some important contracts for the Czar at St Petersburg; and a large order was actually in progress for the Archduke Ferdinand of Serbia when he was murdered – the murder that precipitated the start of the Great War and put out the lamps all over Europe.

In 1913, Arthur Lasenby Liberty had received a knighthood in recognition of his services to the applied and decorative arts of the country. To mark the occasion he was presented with his bust by Sir George Frampton, RA. It was the gift of the textile manufacturers of Great Britain and the Continent – an unique international compliment. It was placed in an embrasure on the staircase at East India House, and customers often enquired the name of the sculptor of King Edward's bust.

The following year the employees of Liberty & Co. presented Sir Arthur with his portrait by Arthur Hacker, RA. At that time, fourteen members of the

High Sheriff of Buckinghamshire, 1899

staff had been with the firm over thirty years, and ninety-eight members over twenty years. There were 1,000 employees in London, over a hundred in Paris, and another hundred in Birmingham. Although it was a public company, it was still very much a family firm. Nearly all the shares were held by the Liberty and Blackmore families, and the atmosphere was still paternalistic. One of the women staff actually described Arthur Liberty as being 'like a dear old father'. That was when he came up early on a Monday morning after a Saturday when the staff outing to The Lee had been drenched by a thunderstorm – he wanted to ask them all personally whether they had caught cold and offer to replace any spoilt clothing. As has been told, he was a pioneer of the Saturday half-holiday movement, and the staff formed societies for all kinds of leisure activities – 'rambles' in the country, dances, cricket, football, tennis, hockey, swimming, harriers. Liberty's 'Lotus Sports Club' was at Perivale, and moved to Merton in 1923, where a large cricket pavilion and bar was built. There was a library of 5,000 books at Chesham House. The staff diningrooms were run by a member of the staff democratically elected each year by secret ballot. He got a 2½ per cent commission on the catering, so it was a coveted position. On the day of the presentation of the portrait, Sir Arthur was ill so unable to be present. Lady Liberty read his speech, and then announced: 'For a long time it has been his wish and the wish of others that some kind of benevolent fund be started for the benefit of the whole of the staff, and he sends a cheque as a nest-egg for the commencement of whatever may be decided upon in that way. The cheque is for £5,000.' *Loud cheering*, as the account in a newspaper reported. The occasion, for which the Central YMCA Hall had been taken, concluded with a concert of songs, piano duets and recitations by members of the Staff.

In this same year, Sir Arthur made his nephew Ivor Stewart his heir, requesting him to take the surname of Stewart-Liberty. Ivor was the son of Sir Arthur's sister Ada, who had married a throat and ear specialist at Nottingham. Later they moved to the Prebendal, Aylesbury; and soon after receiving his MA degree at Christchurch, Oxford, Ivor married Evelyn Phipps, elder daughter of Constantine Phipps, Canon of Christ Church, Oxford, and Vicar of Aylesbury – who the following year resigned the vicarship to accept the vacant living of The Lee. The young Stewart-Libertys were given a house on the green at The Lee, and Ivor began to take over some of his uncle's local commitments. But in less than a year he was in France, an officer in the 2nd Bucks Battalion, Oxfordshire and Buckinghamshire Light Infantry.

Civilian life in London was not affected in the same way in the First World War as the second. Liberty's Spring 1915 catalogue of model dresses, beautifully and expensively produced, was still in two sections: (1) *Costumes Never Out of Fashion*; and (2) *Novelties for the Season*, the first section being printed in the soft colours beloved by the aesthetes. The only concession to the tragic days through which the nation was passing is a note at the end of the catalogue: 'Mourning or half-mourning colours can be substituted for any others.' Customers' suggestions for variations on a model could be carried out, sketches first being sent, free of charge, for approval. The most expensive model in the catalogue is a dinner gown in Dalghali silk-crepe, with crepe de chine stole embroidered in gold and silver, lined with soft silk, 12 gns. Other fashion catalogues issued during 1915 included 'Underwear in Liberty's luxurious and durable washing silks'.

There were still catalogues of Liberty silver-work and Tudric pewter ware; but of course Eastern merchandise was no longer being imported. Raw materials for making civilian goods became more and more scarce, but there were no direct controls as in the Second World War to ensure that inessential goods were not manufactured; nor was there any attempt to control prices until after the war had ended. There was no conscription for the forces, but all the younger members of the staff joined up. An elderly member of the Carpet Department briefly recalled the war years . . . 'The business of the Department was carried on under great difficulties and drawbacks: i.e. greatly reduced staff, uncertain supply of materials, and the natural falling off of orders. But there was no slackness and very little fear as to the result of the War. Every week money was subscribed to provide small luxuries and comforts for the boys at the Front.' The *Liberty Lamp* in many issues during the 1920s carried photographs and obituaries of the men who did not come back. Captain Ivor Stewart-Liberty was awarded the MC and later invalided out, having lost a leg at Merville. He became a director of Liberty & Co. in 1916. His uncle had retired from active administration in 1914. His health was not at all good, and although his final illness at The Lee Manor was a short one, his death on May 11, 1917, was not unexpected.

Sir Arthur was buried in the traditional manner of a squire of the village. The coffin was drawn on a wagon to the village church by workers on the estate, and a vigil kept through the night. The funeral service was attended by representatives of all the societies with which he was associated, from the Buckinghamshire Archaeological Society to the Japan Society, from the Sette of Odd Volumes to the Boy Scouts, and by all the county notabilities from the Earl of Buckinghamshire and the Bishop of Buckingham to the Stationmaster of Great Missenden. The station staff sent a wreath. William Judd, who joined the Founder on the day he opened his first half-shop, was among the 150 members of the staff who came from Regent Street; and 150 school-children sang a hymn at the graveside in The Lee churchyard. Finally, Arthur Lasenby Liberty, Knight, was lowered into the Liberty vault, for which he himself

had chosen the site. A granite gravestone was designed in the Celtic style by Archibald Knox.

If one were attempting an epitaph, one might well adapt something Gordon Selfridge wrote in *The Romance of Commerce*: 'The great merchant must be a world man and not a local man. He must be in touch with all the world of commerce, but he must enjoy the continual gaining of fresh knowledge.' Arthur Lasenby Liberty was a world man *and* a local man. He was a world man in his delight in merchant adventuring and his continual enjoyment of fresh knowledge; and he was a local man in that he returned to his grass roots and became the heart and core of a village community that he himself largely brought into active being.

Sir Arthur left a fortune of £350,000. After legacies to various relatives, personnel at Regent Street, and indoor and outdoor staff at The Lee, he left the residue of his personal property in trust for his nephew Captain Ivor Stewart-Liberty for life, with remainder to his children. The Will concluded: 'I make no legacies to charitable institutions, as I consider that during my life and at my death the State will appropriate an undue proportion of my estate, which has been acquired by personal effort and thrift.' The *Westminster Gazette*, although admitting that during his lifetime Sir Arthur gave generously in many directions, suggested it was 'unfortunate that the Will should be published at a moment when even the richest may be regarded as willing to make some sacrifice for the State'. '*Even* the richest' has a very nasty ring. The *Financial Times* was more sympathetic: 'Evidently the testator's views were long ago embodied in the remonstrance of the individual in the parable – "I feared thee, because thou art an austere man : thou takest up that thou layedst not down, and reapest that thou didst not sow." Even such is the modern "State", war or no war, as every thrifty citizen learns at bitter cost.'

The most bitter cost was felt, in fact, when Ivor Stewart-Liberty died in 1952 at a time when property values were at rock bottom. The Lee Manor, two other residences, some 1,800 of the 3,000 acres, the Lee Gate Inn, ten farms and numerous cottages had to be sold to raise the death duties. It was thought of first importance for the family to retain their 50 per cent of Liberty ordinary and preference shares, so that control of the firm should not be endangered.

Silver chalice designed by Archibald Knox, presented to The Lee church by Liberty staff in London, Paris, and Birmingham

12

TEMPO OF THE TWENTIES
THE NEW BUILDINGS

Liberty & Co. emerged from the war years in astonishingly good shape. The Chairman had said in his Annual Report for the year ended January, 1918: 'From the first Sir Arthur insisted that the finances of this business should be framed on such a conservative and reliable basis that, to use his own words, "it would be able to withstand the shock of a great European war, or some appalling financial crisis, which would create chaos in the money markets of this country". He lived to see his wisdom justified, and I am glad he saw the turn of the tide after we touched our low watermark in the year ended January, 1916, but it is our keen regret that he cannot sign our balance sheet for the year now under review. The turnover has increased in an extraordinary manner – far beyond what we have hoped. The net profit for the year is £61,619 9s 6d – a yield of about 10 per cent on the capital employed.' A dividend of 16 per cent and a bonus of 4 per cent on the Ordinary shares free of tax was declared, and £6,000 set aside for other bonuses.

Then following the Armistice there was a general trade boom which, according to a contributor to the *Liberty Lamp*, 'led to speculation and over-buying which had the natural result in the reaction from which we are all suffering' – he was writing in June 1930. One of the most picturesque speculations was the purchase of a jade mine in Burmah. Jade had always been a speciality of Liberty's. When few other London firms handled it at all, they collected jade amulets and beads of rare colouring and carving from remote localities. In 1919 they produced a little vellum booklet on jade amulets with historical notes of this, to the Chinese people, sacred mineral. It follows that when a mining engineer came into Liberty's in 1923 with a piece of jade the size of a football, he excited acquisitive feelings. This engineer was working for the Burchin Syndicate, who held a jade mine concession at Tawmaw in the Kachin Hills, the stones being stored at Mogaung and worked in Mandalay. Liberty & Co. took shares in the Burchin Syndicate and advanced money to expedite the workings. But because of the depressed state of the market in China, the jade never sold at a reasonable price. About 1933 the stock was sent to Shanghai in an unsuccessful attempt to dispose of it, and it remained there until the outbreak of the Second World War effectively closed the incident.

The Burmese jade mine can be seen as a romantic gesture towards reviving direct ties with the Orient, a gesture in the old merchant adventuring spirit. But that spirit had for the most part been killed, with so much else, by the war. Whereas the history of Liberty's up till 1914 had been one of leadership in taste and fashion, their position in the 1920s was no longer avant-garde. Department buyers who had been too old to fight in the war, now fought on as King Canutes defying the changing tides. They were, in fact, kings over their own territories, with absolute power in the selection of their merchandise, engaging their own staff. They came in at 10 o'clock in the morning and left at 4 o'clock. No direction, let alone initiative, came from the directors. The Board seemed content to let the firm rest on its old reputation.

The old reputation certainly stood it in good stead. Two new social classes had emerged from the war: the New Rich and the New Poor. Old Liberty customers belonged to the New Poor and were therefore, by definition, no longer good customers. But the New Rich, those who had by one means or another profited by the war, were ripe for good pickings. Many had acquired titles as well as riches, and were now hastening to purchase their backgrounds: handsome houses in town and country, where they could entertain in a manner to which they had not previously been accustomed. They were, as Martin Battersby pointed out in *The Decorative Twenties*, a god-send to the luxury trades . . . 'Their lavish spending saved many a firm from bankruptcy in the post-war years. They naturally gravitated to the best-known firms when it came to redecoration and the furnishing of their new homes, and the traditional period schemes with which they were presented were very much to their taste, giving them the feeling of living in "traditional surroundings".' And none presented traditional period schemes more beautifully than Liberty's. In the opinion of one of the staff, it was the fine line drawings, delicately tinted, that sold the scheme. And of course Liberty's had craftsmen and workshops to carry out everything that a desire for the truly traditional demanded: the massive doors and chimney pieces, the pilasters, panelling, banisters, with all the carving done by Seglie, the Italian master-carver who worked for Liberty's. Hand-modelled plaster-work was executed on ceilings and cornices, and hand-wrought metalwork on doors and cupboards. All Liberty's metalwork was by Cecil Ern, who had a forge in a basement in Carnaby Street. Stained-glass work was carried out by experts under Liberty's instructions. For example, the windows of the main hall at Buckhurst Park, home of the oil magnate Sir Henri Deterding, were enriched with Tudor kings and courtiers, while even kitchen and scullery windows had stained-glass panels representing the butcher, the baker, the fishmonger, poulterer, milkmaid, and falconer.

As for furniture, just to take one catalogue of these post-war years is to comprehend all. There are illustrations of two diningrooms, one 'William and Mary Style', the other 'Jacobean Style'. There is a 'Hathaway Suite' in solid oak, and an 'Adam Design Bedroom Suite'. Individual pieces include a 'James II Settee' covered with figured tapestry, a 'Period Charles II' armchair in carved walnut, 'Seventeenth Century Mirrors and Daybeds', 'Sheraton' dining chairs – a splendid selection, in fact, for neo-Georgian residences in the pine woods of Surrey. It is no surprise to be told that the Haddon wallpaper was the most popular at this time and that a moss rose chintz was favoured for bedroom curtains and bedcovers. In carpets, Liberty's own Argram design, made in India, was sold in seven colourways, and in all sizes up to vast 'audience carpet' size.

Clients ordering interior decoration by Liberty's included many who did not slot exactly into the New Rich or the New Poor category. There was the Archbishop of Canterbury at Lambeth Palace, for instance, and Evelyn Laye at her leading-lady's apartment in Park Lane. Also Bernard Shaw. One member of the Liberty Contracts Department had to live for four months at Shaw's unattractive twentieth century house at Ayot St Lawrence while interior work was in progress. The demand for Liberty's furniture was now too great for it all to be made in their own cabinet factory, and much was made to their specifications by High Wycombe firms – that of William Birch had in fact made furniture for Liberty's since the 1890s.

In Paris, the design atmosphere immediately after the Treaty of Versailles was electric compared with that of London. All the art movements that had begun before 1914 sprang alive again; and a thrusting new generation of designers were soon making their mark with furniture, glass, metalwork, textiles, book illustration, posters, fashion drawings and photography. In 1919 Paul Follot and Maurice Dufrene founded *Décoration Intérieure Moderne*, which became known as DIM; and each took positions as directors of decorating departments in Parisian department stores: Dufrene founded '*La Maîtrise*' at the Galeries Lafayette in 1921; Follot directed '*Pomone*' at the Bon Marché from 1923. The culmination of it all was the 1925 *Exposition des Arts décoratifs*.

Familiarly known as the *Arts Déco*, it was this exhibition that gave its name to the Art Deco style. But in spite of the immense interest it aroused on the Continent, it was not until 1928 that any modern French furniture reached London. In that year, Shoolbreds held an exhibition of DIM and other French furniture designers; and the following year Waring & Gillow opened a department of modern French furniture under the direction of Paul Follot and Serge Chermayeff. But Liberty's continued to trudge through the twenties looking backwards. Only the Jewellery Department showed any response to outside influences – such as the influence of American Indian art, a derivative of much Art Deco. Rock crystals, obsidian, Brasilian onyx, were used in modern settings; and all kinds of objects – vases, scent bottles, clocks – appeared in the stepped shape of Aztec temples. The 1922 exhibition of French Colonial Art also had its influence, as did the opening that same year of Tutankamen's tomb. Inevitably there was an eruption of scarabs and other Egyptian motifs.

In fabrics during the 1920s and 1930s, Liberty's were the chief clients of the very active Silver Studio, which now employed a large staff; but the designs they bought were mainly traditional in style, predominantly floral. In furnishing fabrics, a passing gesture towards 'modernism' was to put some traditional cretonne designs onto black backgrounds. But it was Liberty's famous 'Peacock', 'Peony', and 'Pheasant' cretonne designs, already 'classics', that in the late twenties sold in quantities that broke all records – not only Liberty records, but in the trade generally. In dress fabrics, the steadiest seller, then as now, was Tana Lawn, originated by William Haynes Dorell who promoted it with enormous success during his years as head cotton buyer. The name came from Tana Lake in the Sudan, it being made of Sudanese yarn.

The Costume Department, also, maintained a truly traditional atmosphere. Its very name was an anachronism. In the age of jazz and cocktails, open sports cars, night-clubs, dancing mothers and career daughters, an age when the telephone had taken over from the *billet doux* as the medium for affairs and flirtations, Liberty's continued to produce their catalogues in two sections: 'Gowns Never Out of Fashion', illustrating the Grecian and Empire styles favoured by the aesthetes fifty years earlier; and 'Gowns of the New Season', illustrating no awareness that in Paris Chanel had begun to overturn the whole conception of fashion with her accent on uncluttered simplicity, freedom and comfort. It was no longer chic to dress up – but Liberty's still made 'gowns'.

There were, of course, literary and artistic circles where Liberty's still meant something. Indeed, journalists and writers who wished to mock such circles, had only to bring in the word Liberty to conjure up the Bloomsbury

Greek gown in Corie Satin, hand-embroidered with silk and pearls, 25 gns. From 'Costumes Never Out of Fashion' section of Dress Catalogue, 1924

Day Dress in Kamil cloth, with Oriental embroidery. From 'Novelties of the New Season' section of Dress Catalogue, 1924

– or would-be Bloomsbury – scene. Even before the war, according to Susan Lady Tweedsmuir in *Edwardian Lady*, 'stupid people equated intellectual women with those who wore floppy dark green Liberty dresses, strings of beads, and flat heeled shoes'. Somerset Maugham in *Cakes and Ale* (published 1930) wrote of Alroy Kear, rising novelist: 'He joined dining clubs where, in the basement of an hotel in Victoria Street or Holborn, men of letters, young barristers, and ladies in Liberty silks and strings of beads, ate a three-and-sixpenny dinner and discussed art and literature.' And in Dorothy Sayers' *The Documents in the Case*, Jack writes a letter to Bungie dated October 14, 1923: 'I knew we should be asked downstairs to tea. And we've been! Down among the Liberty curtains and the brass Benares ware! Three young women, two bright youths, the local parson and the family. Crockery from Heal's and everything too conscientiously bright . . . No sooner had I got there than I was swept into a discussion about "this wonderful man Einstein!".'

No one could ever dispute the quality of Liberty fabrics, nor the beauty of their silks and brocades. But the prints had been paralysed by success. Hilary Blackmore, who joined the Printworks at Merton in 1926 and was works manager there a few years later, was appalled to find 'not even the colour-ways of designs had been changed between about 1920 and 1924, let alone any new designs introduced . . . it was a dreadful and unhappy period, and I was horrified by the self-satisfaction and atmosphere of laissez-faire of the Board, and by the lack of young people in the shop'.

John Llewellyn was still on the Board (he did not retire until 1935), and since the Founder's death he had had undisputed control over all the artistic aspects of the firm. It seems unbelievable that he, of all people, should have allowed this stagnant state of affairs. The explanation was that his time and thoughts were now almost exclusively occupied with plans for rebuilding. It was upon his 'emphatic advice', according to Bentley, that it was decided to erect a building in Tudor style on Liberty's vast freehold site facing on Great Marlborough Street. In Regent Street, where the land was Crown property, Liberty's had to fall in line with the official plan for the rebuilding of the street.

The first moves in rebuilding had been made as early as 1904, when Norman Shaw was invited by H.M. Office of Woods, Forests, and Land Revenues to prepare designs for Piccadilly Circus and the Quadrant. Shaw's plans proved disconcerting. To quote S. D. Adshead in the December, 1927, issue of the *Architectural World*:

'Mr Shaw, with his wonderful persuasive abilities, foisted upon an expectant group of shopkeepers a style of architecture which, whilst no doubt admir-able as an essay in the fifteenth-century Florentine manner, was at the same time most unsuitable as expressing the modern shop or store. So great were the sacrifices and compromises that had to be made that the fortress character of his Florentine architecture was seriously imperilled; and the Piccadilly Hotel, with its façades to Piccadilly and the Crescent, is the unhappy result. Before their completion Mr Norman Shaw died (in 1912), leaving a group of shopkeepers disappointed and angered with the economic result – and a design or a repeat which it was quite impossible to follow. Mr Shaw expected his shopkeepers to place their goods in caves with rock cut entrances: this would not do.'

It certainly would not do, since the main reason for rebuilding Nash's beautiful street was a commercial reason – to give shopkeepers spacious

modern premises in which they could increase their turnover to meet
increases in rents and rates.

Reginald Blomfield, then President of the RIBA, was asked to find a com-
promise that would preserve the main lines of the Shaw design. Of the result,
the *Architectural World* observed: 'If Mr Norman Shaw's work is reminiscent of a Florentine fortress, the later work of Sir Reginald Blomfield is
reminiscent of the best eighteenth-century monumental architecture of
France. It is Italian, softened and refined.' Well, whether one called it
eighteenth-century monumental French, or Italian Renaissance softened and
refined, Liberty's did not like it. Lofty showrooms and marble pillars they
felt to be out of keeping with their specialist merchandise and the personal
service of experts. They had to comply, but only as far as their property
facing Regent Street was concerned. Harold Blackmore had spent twenty
years buying up adjoining freehold property for the company as it came on
the market, and they now owned an entire island site bounded by Argyll
Place (later Great Marlborough Street), Foubert's Place, Little Marlborough
Street, and Kingly Street. On this site they could go their own way.

Their own way should, they felt, be as far as possible the way of the
Founder. The Tudor period had always had a special appeal to him because
of its association with the great days of merchant adventuring, and with the
ancient guilds of craftsmen. The treasure brought back by seamen and
merchants, and the productions of craftsmen, were sold in the little shops of
Elizabethan London. Liberty's still brought back rich silks, shawls, carpets,
embroideries, jewellery, curios, and porcelain from far countries. They still
had their own workshops and craftsmen, carpenters, carvers, and metal-
workers, by whom all the interior work of a Tudor building could be
executed. It would provide for posterity a building that linked twentieth-
century London with the street architecture of Tudor London, of which
Staple Inn in Holborn is the last large building to remain. Also, the Tudor
style lent itself to small, intimate rooms for display – and the Founder had
always maintained that furniture, furnishings and clothes should be seen in
rooms of similar proportions to those in people's own homes. These were
the given reasons; but stronger than any reasoning was the determination of
John Llewellyn, who was himself under the spell of Tudor because he was
living at Ashwell Court, near Great Missenden – a masterpiece of reproduction Tudor with all its interior woodwork genuine sixteenth century,
coming originally from a monastic building at Blois.

The architects appointed by Liberty's for the Tudor building were
Edwin T. and E. Stanley Hall, father and son. Their design aimed to give the
appearance of a series of shops – a Chester Row – rather than a single great

pile. The timber, oak and teak, came from two old 'two-decker' men-of-war: H.M.S. *Impregnable*, for which 3,040 oaks, each 100 years old, were felled in the New Forest when she was built; and H.M.S. *Hindustan*, which for a long time was one of the 'wooden walls' which formed the *Britannia* at Dartmouth. The *Impregnable*, coincidentally, was exactly the same length as the Argyll Place frontage, and as high out of the water as the distance from the pavement to the eaves of the new building.

The external timber, mortised, tenoned and pegged, is filled and backed with brickwork, the exterior carving being carried out on the site. The stonework is from Portland (London's traditional quarry), chisel-worked from the quarry face to give the rough texture impossible with sawn stone. The roofing tiles were hand-made, the gutters and drain pipes of lead. The original leaded windows each had a small painted picture on one pane. High above the main entrance was set a faithful model of the *Mayflower*, made of gilded copper. And at the doorway are the arms of Henry VIII's six wives, grouped together as they never were in life. The arms of Queen Elizabeth I are on the gable facing Regent Street.

Inside, the design is of a series of deep galleries, four storeys high, grouped around three wells resembling the courtyards of old English inns. There are carved balustrades, linen-fold panelling, oak staircases, floors made from the deck timbers of the old men-of-war, heraldry introduced into the decoration to add colour: in the roof of the East Central Gallery there are six shields, those of Ben Jonson, Sir Thomas More, Sir Philip Sidney, Bacon, George Herbert, and Shakespeare. A small panelled room on the ground floor, with a heavy iron gate kept locked, is the 'Fine Jewellery Room', a holy of holies where important customers (including Queen Mary) used to be shown rare pieces. There was a special sofa for Queen Mary, and this, with the rest of the original furniture once scattered, has now been found and returned to the Fine Jewellery Room. In the basement there was a tea-room – rather like a castle dungeon with thick stone walls and massive pillars. A customer once asked a salesman in the main shop to direct her to the tea-room in the crypt. But the china used was considered extremely modern because it was Moorcroft's plain Blue Tableware. William Moorcroft was a friend of the Liberty family, and his second wife was a Lasenby. Liberty & Co. owned half his pottery. Until 1913 he had been with James Macintyre of Burslem, who from about 1900 supplied Liberty's with Moorcroft's Florian Ware. He made all their commemorative mugs, including some designed by Arthur Liberty himself.

The Tudor building contractors were Higgs & Hill, founded in 1874 and

INTERIOR DETAIL, FIRST FLOOR

builders of many important London properties, amongst them the Tate Gallery, India House, Victoria Station, Chelsea Barracks, Holy Trinity Church, Sloane Square, Park Lane Hotel, Peter Robinson, Dickins & Jones, Harvey Nichols, Fulham Power Station. The Tudor building was a rare opportunity for their joiners, carpenters, and other craftsmen to employ their skills to the full; and when it was finished, they asked if they might show their families round. The firm had never had a similar request before. Mr Ronald Hill, formerly chairman of his family company, remembers being taken as a boy to see the building in progress and watching the men adzing the timbers. He says the foreman, J. Corfield, who like his father before him had worked all his life with the firm, was trained as a carpenter, and carried enormous responsibilities in those days when the site staff was minimal. Mr Hill recalls also that a year or two later his firm built a large Tudor-style house in Headley, Epsom, for the Hon. Geoffrey Cunliffe . . . 'He must have been a great admirer of Liberty's Tudor shop, as he employed the same architect as well as the same builder.'

The architectural critics of the day were at a loss for the right words. Sydney Kitson in the *Architectural World* toiled away with an elaborate analogy about what would happen 'if Queen Elizabeth should choose to return and haunt the shopping centre of modern London in the full splendour of her traditional dress'. He allowed that 'the public will admire the quaint-ness of the design and the obvious charm of the craftsmanship. It will recog-nise the ingenuity and skill with which the architects have carried out their instructions'. Then he goes on, 'I do not intend to answer the question as to whether such a building is calculated to advance the art of architecture. It is clothed in Elizabethan dress, but constructed to comply with the bye-laws of the twentieth century. Its accessories, such as carved barge-boards, lead rain-water heads, and painted glass, have doubtless given greater pleasure in the doing to numerous craftsmen than such men would have obtained in modern "classical" work.' Modern 'classical' has never been so derided as 'mock Tudor'.

It was a happy thought to ask William Judd to open the Tudor building – William Judd who had thrown in his lot with Arthur Liberty when he opened his first half-shop. And on October 24th of the following year, William Judd was called upon again – this time to open the newly built East India House on Regent Street. He wrote in the *Liberty Lamp* : 'I was met by a sea of happy smiling faces and congratulations. Mr Henley then handed me the key with which I opened the door – to be met by a great shout and dear Miss Flood called out in a loud clear voice "Good luck!", and Mr Foster then called for three cheers for the Company's success and I felt very grateful for the honour that was bestowed on me to have opened such a beautiful building, which has no equal.' Dear Miss Flood was Miss Jessie Flood, who worked in the scarf department, and was the last of the sales ladies to be dressed in a Liberty gown. At one time they all wore aesthetic gowns, with Liberty silk bandeaux tied around their heads. Although William Judd was officially retired at this time, seven years later there is a paragraph in the *Liberty Lamp* of January, 1932, congratulating him on his 85th birthday, and saying, 'William Judd still comes to the Furniture Department so dear to his heart each day.' There was no stopping him.

The new East India House, conforming to the approved style for Regent Street, was designed by the same architects and constructed by the same builders as the Tudor shop. The only feature to arouse contemporary controversy was the frieze, 115 feet long, surmounting the central curved recess of the façade. Designed by Edwin T. Hall and sculptured by Charles L. J. Doman and Thomas J. Clapperton, it is a *tour de force* with a typically Victorian theme . . . the wealth of far countries is being borne by camel, elephant, and ship to Great Britain, which is represented by a statue of Britannia. Surmounting the frieze and breaking the skyline, three figures watch the mercantile pageant below. These figures are so lifelike, that to anyone who happens to cast his eyes skyward from the opposite side of Regent Street, there appear to be actual people on the roof peering over. The *Architectural World* of December, 1927, in an article upon the new Regent Street, had no qualms in expressing unqualified admiration of East India House:

'In Liberty's ground storey we read a solemnity, and almost bank-like strength and well-being. Here is character unmistakable, the indication of an Empire trade, wide spans suggesting an imperial breadth of commerce, the Royal arms as a discreetly arrogant hallmark of distinction. The wares of the Orient and Occident look well in their sober black framework, and the windows seem to have plate-glass of an almost luscious thickness and polish. The shop-fronts of Liberty's in Regent Street suggest a top-hatted and fur-coated wealth, a directorate courteous, polished, very English and patriotic, always open for business on the basis of quality, trust, and confidence.'

It was not only the directorate that was courteous and polished. The commissionaires (two on each door) and the cicerones, as the shopwalkers were called, were the acme of polished aplomb. There was A. W. Foster who was a cicerone from 1893 until 1929, always dressed in a light grey frock coat and beautifully tied cravat. Another cicerone was nicknamed The Count by the staff, and is evocatively described in a letter from C. Stilliard:

'We had a most swagger shopwalker on the Marlborough Street door. Tall, and a figure which suggested corsets, a little pointed beard, and altogether with a most aristocratic bearing and address. Once when the carpets were up and the parquet flooring was highly polished, he was conducting some ladies in his most princely manner and stepped off the drugget, and came down whallop on his back!! I, with my youthful frivolity, chose this moment to present him with a bill to sign whilst he lay on his back!!! He never loved me after.'

The floors and other woodwork were all polished at night by a small force of ex-naval ratings and Marines, under the command of Mr Rundle, ex-bosun.

There were also lady cicerones. An American business man who visited Liberty's wrote in the *Chicago Daily News*: 'I was met at the doorway by a gray-haired, alert, beautifully gowned lady, smiling and gracious as a princess . . . more like a friendly hostess than a cold, haughty, and mechanical shopwalker.' This would have been Miss Theresa Hinds, perhaps not so friendly to staff as to customers, since Guy Bentley refers to 'Miss Hinds who dominates the Entrance Showrooms'. Stanley Porter (who joined Liberty's in 1927) remembers her as having a Gibson Girl figure . . . 'She wore a long dress of brown velvet, and used to kick the train on one side as she turned corners. She was a fantastic saleswoman, but would never serve lady customers, only the gentlemen.' One American thought she was Mrs Liberty. Mr Porter also remembers Miss Heighton of the Costume Department, who dressed as Elizabeth 1. At this time the length of fashionable skirts was only just to the knee – the shortest skirts in the history of fashion until the mini-skirts of the 1960s.

The final addition to the new buildings was a three-storey arched bridge with enclosed passages over Kingly Street to connect East India House with the Tudor shop. It has a clock designed by E. P. Roberts of Liberty's cabinet studios and made by Mr Hope-Jones, then Chairman of the British Horological Institution. Forming the spandrels of the clock face are four winged heads, representing the Four Winds. Morning is symbolised by a crowing cock and a rising sun; night by an owl and the moon. In a recess above, at each chiming of the hour, St George and the Dragon fight it out. Above, a leaded window is crowned by a cornice supported by two grotesque figures. Quite a clock. Nor has Father Time been left out: he is on the keystone of the arch with an inscription:

> No minute gone comes ever back again,
> Take heed and see ye nothing do in vain.

Who would say now that the Tudor building had been done in vain? For fifty years it has been one of the sights of London for visitors; and Londoners themselves have come to regard it with the greatest affection. If it were ever threatened with demolition, a whole army of preservationists would rise up and call it sacred. But there is no danger. It has a preservation order, and is listed as a building of architectural interest.

13

FROM THE GENERAL STRIKE
TO WORLD WAR II

It was a relief to shopkeepers and shoppers alike when the rebuilding of Regent Street was finished. An account in the *Financial World* of June 21, 1924, gives an idea of what they had endured:

'No doubt it will be a very magnificent street – one of the finest streets in Europe – with much improved facilities for carrying on trade; but while the reconstruction is going on the public don't consider it safe to promenade there, in as much as huge boulders of stone, ironwork girders and temporary bridges are a cause of grave apprehension, if not of actual danger, to pedestrians. The traffic is almost daily at a standstill owing to the huge motor lorries loaded with girders, bricks, etc., and motor cars are not allowed to remain in Regent Street, thus causing serious inconvenience to customers.'

The chaos continued for more than two years after that, but at last the new Regent Street was formally opened by King George v and Queen Mary on June 24, 1927. They drove up the decorated street in an open carriage, and photographs show the pavements thick with cheering crowds. No doubt many people were able to be there because they were unemployed – it was only a year after the General Strike. Londoners when they are short of bread have, like the Romans, all the more appetite for circuses.

To many people, it must be admitted, the General Strike itself had been a bit of a lark, a break from routine, the chance of a lifetime to drive trains or buses, to unload ships or play policeman. Since 1921 there had been a section of the Metropolitan Special Constabulary Reserve composed of some sixty men from Liberty's; also some units made up of men from Bourne & Hollingsworth, Jay's, and other West End firms who were members of the London Employers' Association. There were parades in Hyde Park on State occasions, and on Armistice Day at the Cenotaph. Now they had the chance to do something more than parading. A 'SPECIAL' issue of the *Liberty Lamp*

THE 'LIBERTY' LAMP

Vol. II.   THE GREAT STRIKE, 1926.   EXTRA.

OUR " SPECIAL" NUMBER.

tells how the London Business Houses, Division 2, of the Special Police was called to action:

'On the eventful Monday, 3rd May, 1926, when the great catastrophe came, the services of the Specials were needed by the State. Our men were ready uniformed and equipped and we started the task of recruiting, attesting and equipping those who at the call of need were anxious to help the Government in the continuance of law and order. A commencement was made on Wednesday, May 5th, when Capt. Stewart-Liberty, assisted by Sir James Boyton (who has now, alas, passed to the great majority) swore in some 50 men in the Orderly Room that had been improvised at 32 Kingly Street.

'On Thursday more and more men came forward for attestation and we had our first call for emergency duty, when 30 of our men were sent to Bow Street Police Station from whence they were detailed for various duties at Somerset House, the *Morning Post* office, etc. From then onwards there was a continual stream of men for attestation and equipment. In some cases two magistrates attended at Marlborough Street Police Court and at Scotland Yard, where magistrates were sitting all day for the purpose. One hundred and fifty Liberty employees formed A Company of the Division. Each day we were called to send men to Limehouse, Poplar, Borough, etc. and to provide their transport – lorries, vans and cars were lent by friends. The work Mr Hubert Reichholz did with his little Amilcar was phenomenal; from early morning till late night he was always ready. Once he brought our Commander from Brondesbury to Regent Street in four minutes.

'Empty rooms on the first floor of 208 Regent Street were utilised as a muster-room, canteen and recreation room, and mattresses provided for sleeping. Messrs F. J. Lyons & Co. and Messrs Bourne & Hollingsworth each provided quarters in their premises. Fortunately there were no casualties among our men whilst on duty, though they were often working in neighbourhoods where serious troubles occurred.'

The most sensational sortie seems to have been in a *British Gazette* newsprint convoy from the *Morning Post* offices to Plymouth, the first night being spent in a steam lorry whose maximum speed was 5 mph and which had to be refilled with water every twelve miles.

When the strike was over, a Divisional dinner was held at Lyons' Corner House, at the invitation of Mr Blackmore, Mr J. Bourne and Mr A. L. Lyons . . . 'There were speeches, songs and toasts. *Land of Hope and Glory* was sung by Miss D. Radford, assisted in the second chorus by the orchestra and the entire assembly.'

*   *   *   *   *

In the early 1920s, Paul St G. Perrott, designer and manager of the Costume Department at Regent Street, was transferred to the Paris branch, which was now moved from the avenue de l'Opéra to the boulevard des Capucines. There were over a hundred employees and five workrooms. French issues of the *Liberty Lamp* reported on the gaieties of champagne, jazz and fancy dress in the workrooms on St Catherine's Day, the annual fête day of Parisian midinettes; and Mr Perrott wrote of the *Bal de la Couture* in the April, 1926, issue. It was held at the Opéra, and all the loges were taken by famous couturiers (he mentions Drécoll, Lanvin, Beer, Charlotte, Poiret, Redfern, and Lucile – the last two being English, with Paris branches). The finale was a *défile de mannequins* from the *Grandes Maisons* . . . 'The gowns were sensational to a degree. One mannequin, among a bevy in evening gowns, was '*habillée entièrement en smocking*' – she must surely have been from the Maison Liberty. Another mannequin 'carried the oriental dreams of Monsieur Poiret to the pitch of a tawny brown make-up and golden nail-protectors many inches in length'. He reported that 'skirts and hair are shorter than ever', and one is reminded that this was the time of the Eton crop, flat chests, and knee-short waistless dresses.

In August, 1927, Mr Perrott wrote of 'the newly transformed and redecorated salons in the Paris House':

'The atmosphere is essentially French. The elaborate gilded and sculptured cornice, the massive classic columns, the tall arched windows, the well-drawn lines, and above all the symmetry, all these combine to recall the past glories of eighteenth-century France. The entrance to the fitting-rooms is topped by an artistically-mounted clock, and flanked by heavy marble columns; on either side, little recesses make an admirable background for a bright hued mantle or gown. A little polygon-shaped salon is peculiarly charming. It has three tall windows, whose crossed curtains of creamy silk recall the period of Marie Antoinette. A vast mirror ornamented with gilt studs gives an effect of considerable perspective as the pretty mannequins pass before it.'

These were the couture salons on the first floor; and there was also the children's salon where Liberty smocks and dresses in the Kate Greenaway style could be ordered. On the ground floor a boutique sold Liberty scarves, shawls, cushions, Indian bedcovers, and oriental *objets de fantaisie*. From the memoirs of Céleste Albaret, Proust's housekeeper, published under the title of *Monsieur Proust*, we know they sold neck-ties for men . . . '*A un certain moment, il avait porté des lavallières, achetées chez Liberty; mais il les avait abandonnées; je ne les ai vues que dans une boite où il les gardait.*' Another reference is to Proust's purchase of a duvet . . . '*Rangé dans une armoire, il y avait bien aussi un duvet, qu'il s'était fait faire spécialement à grand frais chez Liberty, boulevard des Capucines, mais qu'il avait vite écarté parceque la plume était mauvaise pour son asthme.*' The boutique also sold the famous Liberty silks by the yard. Madame Véra, who was Balenciaga's *première vendeuse* in later years, remembers when she first arrived in Paris from Russia after the Revolution, seeing the Liberty windows hung from ceiling to floor with beautiful silks.

During the 1920s, much money was spent by visiting Americans in Paris, and much, much more by American garment manufacturers on couture models for copying. After the Wall Street crash of 1929, 10,000 work-people in Paris fashion became unemployed. The Maison Liberty managed to carry on until 1932, when new tariffs compelled it to close. It was John Llewellyn's son Paul who supervised the sad closure. He had served through the war in the Welsh Guards, been severely wounded and awarded the MC. Afterwards, he was appointed Equerry to the Prince of Wales, but he never fully recovered from his wounds, and in 1921 resigned his commission to join Liberty's. He became manager of the printworks at Merton, and a director of the company in 1929.

It was probably in order to keep some ties with Paris that Paul Poiret was engaged to design dress collections for Liberty's in Regent Street. No one on the Board realised that the celebrated avant-gardiste was no longer avant-

Paul Poiret. Sketch by Cecil Beaton. Reproduced from *The Glass of Fashion* by courtesy of Sir Cecil Beaton

garde. In point of fact, as a couturier he was finished. In 1924 he had been reduced to selling his name and talents to a company which financed a new Poiret couture house at 1 Rond-Point des Champs Elysées. But Poiret could not, or would not, discipline his designing to the new social climate, and the house closed in 1929. As his biographer Palmer White says, 'Poiret epitomised a period when a woman dressed to enhance her personal beauty, to amuse herself, to widen the range of her coquetry. Now women dressed to follow a career. Naturally, Poiret understood this evolution. But he felt that the new trend was only temporary, and was convinced that he could channel it back into his way of more opulent beauty. He failed to understand the irrevocability of the change.' [1] Liberty's, also, had failed to understand it.

Sir Cecil Beaton in *The Glass of Fashion* relates a story told to him by Poiret's nephew, Jean Bongard, about a contract with Liberty's. In the early thirties, when the designer was living in two top floors of the Salle Pleyel, with no money to pay the rent, he took his uncle out to lunch. Poiret spoke of some business men who were coming later that day from Liberty's in London 'to discuss a transaction whereby he would design some prints for mass copy and cheap distribution in England, receiving 10,000 francs in advance for his work'. On the strength of this, he invited his nephew to lunch the next day. When Bongard arrived, he found Poiret had spent the entire 10,000 francs on a telescope to watch the stars and a refrigerator in

[1] *Poiret* by Palmer White. Studio Vista, 1973.

which were 'innumerable chilled bottles of champagne'. They drank the champagne and conveniently forgot the lunch. Did Poiret also conveniently forget to design the fabrics for which the money was advanced? There is no record of them. It seems likely that Jean Bongard was mistaken in saying the contract was to design fabrics, and that the advance was on his appointment to design dress collections for Liberty's. This he undoubtedly did. An IMPORTANT ANNOUNCEMENT was sent out to customers, dated April, 1932:

'Liberty's of Regent Street, London, and Boulevard des Capucines, Paris. On May 2nd we are inaugurating A MODEL GOWN DEPARTMENT, when a fresh collection of new Models executed under the direct supervision of a Paris dress designer will be shown at extremely attractive prices and made in the well-known Liberty materials. Our workrooms and, in fact, everything to do with our dress departments are being re-organised.'

Poiret must have designed at least four collections for Liberty's, two Spring and two Autumn, as there exists in the Liberty archives an invitation to a Dress Parade on October 3, 4 and 5, 1933:

'Whether it be the exclusive model gown for the formal occasion, or the less expensive dress for practical wear, there are pleasant surprises in store at Liberty's. For not only do the creations of Paul Poiret gratify those who seek, above all, artistic perfection, but the models fashioned by our own expert designers and dressmakers delight those in search of elegance at a price which is, to say the least, quite discreet.'

This implies that the prices of the Poiret models were, to say the least, indiscreet. As, indeed, was the life style of the man, who always conducted himself as though on top of the world even when he was at the end of his resources. A senior member of Liberty's staff remembers Poiret, a small man with a jaunty beard clad in velvet jacket and peach coloured trousers with a stripe down the leg – strutting through the store like a bantam, as though cock of the roost. Palmer White's biography does not include any Liberty episode, but we learn from it that Poiret was applying for unemployment relief the following year.

The dressmaking workrooms at Liberty's were well equipped to make the most extravagant clothes that Poiret could conceive. There was an embroidery room, a pleating room, and a model room where Paul St G. Perrot, back from the Paris House, cut out his dresses on the model girls. There was also a French Room where, besides the Poiret models, copies of models from

French couture houses were made – Liberty buyers went to the Paris collections, and ordered *toiles* or paper patterns, as well as some actual models for line by line copying. There were also no less than twelve workrooms making children's clothes, under the direction of Miss Gravet: smocked party dresses and Harris tweed coats were their forte, and they made uniforms for a great many exclusive schools.

Lilian Hughes (later Mrs Sutton, and still with the firm) joined Liberty's in 1930 as an apprentice hand at 6s a week, when there were sixty to eighty girls in the workrooms. Promotion was slow and training thorough. After one year, an apprentice became an improver at 12s a week; after two years she would be a junior hand's jobber at 17s 10d; the next year she became a junior hand at 24s; then a top junior hand at 27s 10d. They had one half-day free a week, and on three evenings a week went to evening school. Lilian Hughes attended the Barrett Street Training College for four years, where she took the City and Guilds examinations. The ultimate top job was that of Head Fitter: still with a low wage but, as Mrs Sutton says, 'Obviously you worked for pleasure, not for profit. The materials were so beautiful, and it was sacrilege to me not to get a pattern to flow round.' The last of the maker workrooms was closed in 1971, and now there are only six to eight alteration hands – *experienced* hands, Mrs Sutton emphasises.

Promotion was also slow on the sales floors. Mr Frank Gouldstone, who is still with the firm, joined the Silk Department in 1927 as one of three boys whose job it was to measure remnants and put stock away. He spent as much time as he could working behind the scenes in the stockroom with the buyers, and learning from John Llewellyn whose taste and knowledge he greatly admired . . . 'He dressed like an artist, a real Bohemian.' When he was nineteen, Frank Gouldstone was given a bill book and started to serve. There were twelve salesmen in the department, and since serving was in order of seniority there had to be eleven customers being served before he got a chance . . . 'It was hard times then – low wages and high commission – you had to sell to make a living.' But in spite of the financial depression, Marlborough Street was still lined with limousines in the middle of the morning, with waiting chauffeurs, and sometimes footmen as well: . . . 'It was a different type of customer then. If she said, "Have it sent, please", you couldn't ask her name, you were expected to know it. It was a very good class of tourist trade as well, Indian Maharajahs, rich South Americans. Nobody from the Continent in the 1930s, they were too poor. And the Americans had stopped coming after the Wall Street crash. At the January and July sales there was a different type of customer altogether, the sort who asked if things would wear and wash well.'

At the world slump in 1930, one man out of every department had to go, and it was Mr Gouldstone who went from Silks. But a traveller was being retired in the Trade Room, so he took on that job, calling on couture houses to show the latest ranges of fabrics. He would call on Worth, Madame Isabelle, Handley Seymour, Norman Hartnell, Hardy Amies. 'We showed them exclusive lines, unobtainable elsewhere. We always refused to sell to the ready-to-wear, however much they asked.

'Queen Mary used to come to the shop sometimes, and she was always served by Mr Barbassio. Any fabric she chose had to be taken straight out of the range. We made her a beautiful dress for a Command Performance, and she was so pleased with it that Mr Barbassio received an invitation for the Royal evening. We supplied quantities of Tana Lawn for Princess Elizabeth and Princess Margaret when they were children. We had a message once to take some lace to Marlborough House for their grandmother to choose for them to wear at the Coronation of George VI. We had very special hand-made Honiton lace, but to give more choice, I took along some machine-made Chantilly as well. Of course I told Queen Mary it was machine lace, but she would have it. She wouldn't spend more than £40. Mr Griffin was furious that I'd taken the machine-made.' This was Charley Griffin, buyer of the Miscellaneous Department and a Liberty relative. He was once mistaken for a customer by a new young salesman, who asked him if he was looking for the way out. 'Look here, my boy,' he replied, 'I've been in this place for forty years and haven't found the way out yet!'

There was no separate Liberty wholesale company until 1939; but even before 1900 Liberty's were selling dress and furnishing fabrics, also silk scarves and squares, at wholesale prices to other shopkeepers. Trade purchasers just went round the store to see what was available and then bought at discount prices. The first European shop to buy fabrics and furnishings in quantity from Liberty's was Metz of Amsterdam and The Hague, starting in 1890. In Berlin and Vienna, Liberty sold to E. Braun. In Paris, they had their own Maison Liberty. Important early customers in the USA were McCutcheons and Best of New York, Wanamakers of New York and Philadelphia, Stearne's of Boston, and the White House in San Francisco. Trimingham's in Bermuda began to be a customer in 1912, and Myers Emporium of Melbourne in 1922, Robert Simpson's Co. of Canada in 1927, and Ballantyne's of Christchurch, New Zealand, in 1935. A list of British towns with Liberty agents in 1890 was given in Chapter 7; and by the turn of the century Jenners of Edinburgh, Bainbridge of Newcastle, Jolly's of Bath and Bristol, Cavendish House, Cheltenham, and Beaths of Canterbury could all be added. The last two named had complete Liberty departments,

Delivery van of Metz & Co. of Amsterdam and The Hague, early 1920s

and issued catalogues linking their names with Liberty. For example, the Winter Sale catalogue of Cavendish House in December, 1909, had a page devoted to Liberty wares: fabrics, scarves, Indian printed bedcovers, cushions, table-covers, Japanese inlaid tables, lacquer trays, tea-stands, embroidered draught screens, Liberty garden and summer hats, panama hats, felt hats. In Birmingham there had been a branch of Liberty's since 1887. In Manchester a Liberty branch opened in 1924 in St Ann's Street. It moved to new premises at 16–18 King Street in 1955, where it still is.

Once the world slump was over, Americans and other foreign visitors began coming back to London. The Liberty buyers happily stocked up to the hilt. Thus when war broke out in 1939 there were vast stocks in hand. Mr Dorell of Tana Lawn fame, by then a director, lived at Croydon and had the bright idea of renting a little shop there to sell Liberty specialities. It was quite a success, since once the bombing started people began to shop locally instead of going to the West End. In fact, the overbuying of the late 1930s served the firm well. For example, an enormous consignment of leather handbags from Italy lasted throughout the war: the use of real leather was not permitted for civilian goods, so good handbags were unobtainable elsewhere. Many other raw materials were also prohibited and in April, 1940, the first Limitation of Supplies Order imposed restrictions on cotton, rayon, and linen goods. In June, 1941, clothes rationing came into force, and in the following spring austerity regulations were imposed on all clothing in order to save labour as well as materials. Trimmings were restricted, as were the number of pleats, seams, buttons, the width of sleeves, belts, hems and collars. When Norman Hartnell and Hardy Amies designed some 'utility' styles for mass manufacture, everyone thought they were splendid value; and the word utility, according to the President of the Board of Trade, became a 'noble title'.

From August, 1942, all manufacture of furniture was prohibited except twenty-two items, each with a prescribed timber content. Two qualities and three designs were specified for each item. From June, 1942, domestic pottery was restricted to a very narrow range, undecorated; some plain white cups were even made without handles. From all this, and remembering that much of Liberty's merchandise used to be imported from far countries, it can be seen that normal business was in total abeyance. The staff dwindled as the age limit for war service was raised, and the remainder worked a rota of fire-watching, day and night, men and women. The tea-room in the 'crypt' was turned into a canteen for those on Air Raid Precautions duties. Harold Blackmore, Chairman since 1936, was on duty with his squad dealing with incendiaries on the roof, two nights on and two nights off, during the whole of the war.

Liberty's were lucky. Whereas John Lewis received a direct hit and their Oxford Street building was completely burned down, the nearest bomb to Liberty's was in Conduit Street. This broke all the windows of East India House, and another direct hit on the Great Marlborough Street premises of the International Dental Companies broke the windows of the Liberty Counting House. Next morning the floor of the Sold Ledger Office was carpeted with false teeth – the only time, observed the financial director, that actual teeth were put into Liberty's debt-collecting arrangements.

Exterior detail of
Tudor Building

14

POST-WAR RENAISSANCE
INTO THE SEVENTIES

The end of the war did not bring the end of wartime restrictions. *Punch*, reflecting the day-to-day life of the British people, based its cartoons and jokes on such basically unfunny subjects as the housing shortage, electricity cuts, empty grates, empty petrol tanks, empty shops. Some austerity regulations were even tightened. Shortage of labour in the textile mills caused a cut in the clothing ration; shortage of timber caused more rigorous priorities on dockets for utility furniture. China and pottery for the home market remained plain white, decorated was for export only. All luxury fashion goods, such as cashmere sweaters and nylon stockings, were creamed off for export. Indeed, 'for export only' became a catch phrase, successor to 'Don't you know there's a war on?'

Yet the atmosphere at Liberty's was much brisker than it had been in the trade boom that immediately succeeded the First World War. Change was in the air, and more young men were coming back into the business than had returned after 1918. Amongst them were Hilary Blackmore, the Chairman's son, and Arthur Stewart-Liberty, whose father became Chairman upon Harold Blackmore's retirement in 1950. These two first cousins, great-nephews of the Founder, symbolised the young generation that would be responsible for lifting Liberty's into the second half of the twentieth century. Ironically, the main obstacle to a modern image was Liberty's long-established reputation. Old faithful customers wanted to buy their old favourite fabrics, and resented any changes in the departments. It would be contrary to the very spirit of Liberty's to betray the faithful; but these were customers who, in the course of nature, would soon die out. In June, 1946, the Board issued a policy statement to the staff, which included the point that 'although we have a good connection in the typical "Liberty's" and precious types of goods, a new factor is now coming into play. Most of the wartime customers were of necessity middle-aged, as the younger generations were otherwise engaged. The latter are now rapidly being released into civilian life; they will become the customers of those shopkeepers who show most enterprise in catering for their taste. Each department should therefore carry a percentage of goods that are contemporary in feeling'. And the Board undertook to 'subsidise' experimental lines: those that proved unsuccessful would not be debited to the department concerned, but to a separate company account.

That same month, Eric E. Lucking was appointed to take charge of display. Liberty's had never had a special display man before, the windows allocated to each department being dressed by the department's salesmen. Lucking was given a free rein to devise composite windows, taking complementary merchandise from different departments, and his witty displays had an electric effect after wartime dreariness. They delighted passers-by, and brought Liberty's a great deal of editorial notice. The businessmen's magazine *Fortune* (April, 1951) wrote:

'E. E. Lucking, a leading light in the modern display world, makes of each window a unified composition of form and colour, symbolic, sophisticated, classically simple or dreamily fantastic, sometimes bizarre and surrealist, but always original and imparting to the West End something of that inventive chic belonging to the smartest Continental houses.'

Lucking himself says he needed more ingenuity than genius to conjure up those first chic windows. To achieve any sense of modernity, he had first to get rid of the walnut panelling at the back of the windows. Timber was rationed, cloth was rationed; but by grubbing around Soho sheds, he got together a quantity of wooden battens and carried them back on his shoulder to Regent Street. With these he made screens, stretching blackout material over them and spray-painting it white. There were no display figures to be had, so he devised them out of wire, straw, anything he could lay his hands on. He made masks for faces, and sometimes 'heads' of bunches of flowers. He used Lyn Chadwick mobiles and, at Christmas, long tendrils with hands offered presents. The central figure of one of his most arresting windows was a giraffe with Liberty scarves knotted all the way down its neck. The men's department was being extended to carry outerwear as well as the shirts, ties and dressing-gowns that were its traditional stock; and as soon as display figures became available, Liberty's windows were some of the first in London to have men and girl models together – a daring innovation at the time. Only once was a Lucking display censored. He had designed a pure white window for the week of Princess Elizabeth's wedding. To make more impact by contrast, he dressed the adjacent window entirely with black lingerie. This was considered by the Board to be in bad taste.

Display figures by Phyllis Richards in Eric Lucking's studio

Fortnightly meetings were set up at which display staff, designers, and department buyers discussed the co-ordination of displays and events throughout the store. One original enterprise was an exhibition held in the summer of 1952 by students of the Royal College of Art – ceramics, furniture, and fabrics – arranged under the direction of Sir Hugh Casson. In those days, the work of art college students received far less attention and publicity than it does now, far less sponsorship by textile firms, manufacturers, and fashion houses in the way of design competitions and travel scholarships. This exhibition, which brought students into touch with future employers and the buying public, was considered such a success that another was held the following year.

In post-war England, design had become a much discussed subject. Not since the last decades of the previous century had so much talk gone on about architecture and town planning, street 'furniture', interior decoration, household things of everyday use. Corbusier's dictum that houses should be machines for living in was repeated as gospel, and 'fitness for purpose' was the cliché on everybody's lips. It was a far cry from art for art's sake; but there was a sincere belief that things could be fit for their purpose and at the same time aesthetically acceptable. The Design and Industries Association was transfused with fresh vigour. Founded as far back as 1915, it had never been of great influence. But now, faced with a plastic, man-made fibre future, manufacturers and industrialists joined artists, designers, and retailers in attempting to ensure that the new discoveries of science should be functionally deployed in a pleasing manner. The Scandinavian countries were coming forward with a clean, cool look in furniture and furnishings; and post-war Italy, creatively resurgent, shone with the most brilliant designers. In England, there had been Milner Gray's 'Design for the Home' exhibition held by the Council for the Encouragement of Music and the Arts; the following year the Council of Industrial Design held their 'Britain Can Make It' exhibition, and a Design and Research Centre was set up for the gold, silver, and jewellery industries. With the 1951 Festival of Britain on the South Bank alongside the newly built Festival Hall, Britain for the first time since the beginning of the century became a place to visit for everyone involved in industrial design and the applied arts.

It was in this design climate that Liberty's opened in 1950 a department for modern furniture, and mounted a series of exhibitions: Venini hand-blown glass from Murano; furniture, lamps, cutlery, china and glass from West Germany; Bernard Leach pottery; the first Finnish bentwood birch furniture by Alvar Aalto that became modern 'classics'; also from Finland, the glasswork of Tapio Wirkkala and Kai Franck; from Denmark, furniture by Finn Juhl, Arne Jacobsen, and Kay Bojesen; from Italy, furniture by Gio Ponti. In fashion, also, a new era had started with the 'Young Liberty' department opened in 1949. It was designed by Hulme Chadwick, designer of aircraft interiors. To the loudly expressed horror of some members of the staff, he put in a false ceiling to cover the beams in one of the galleries of the Tudor shop, and concealed the Elizabethan windows by converting them into modishly lit display bays. His colour scheme was primrose, grey and green, with fittings in Sapele mahogany and Avodiré – a rare, golden-yellow South African wood. At least the Liberty tradition was upheld in the quality of the materials used. Although 'Young Liberty' had its own young buyer, every fashion and accessory department in the store was invited to contribute merchandise, and this had the effect of alerting all buyers to the new spirit of youth that was being encouraged.

The greatest organisational changes were in the important area of fabrics. An Advisory Design Committee was set up, and the absolute power of the department buyers ended absolutely. Liberty & Co. (Wholesale) Ltd was given its own separate organisation to design and produce printed fabrics, to programme and style its products for overseas markets as well as the Regent Street shop. In the shop itself, exports were promoted by opening a Retail Export section in each department. In the first tourist season after the war, USA visitors spent nearly 200,000 dollars. Inevitably, it was the old favourites they went for: Tana Lawn, printed linens and cretonnes, fine wool fabrics and silks, men's ties and dressing-gowns . . . anything modern, they said, they could get at home. They were fascinated by a demonstration of block printing set up in the store, watching the building up of the design on the silk – at least twenty-five block impressions being required for each scarf.

It was, alas, the demonstration of a dying craft. Only consider: it used to take two weeks to make a block, and for one of the typical Indian shawl designs twenty-seven blocks were required. Today that would mean a cost of about £3,000 for the blocks alone, if anyone could be found to make them. Then hand-printing the shawl in the sixty block lays necessary would take over a day. With piece goods, only 30 yards could be produced in a day, compared with about 180 yards by silk-screen printing, and 300 yards an *hour* by machine printing. Freddie Sears, who retires this year, was the last to do block-printing for Liberty's – his father worked for the Littlers at Merton from the age of 13 to 75 years, and Freddie started his seven-year apprenticeship in 1924. He remembers when there were fifty-two block-printers working for Liberty's. When Gustav Weiner, who was previously with Ascher, joined the print-works in the mid-1950s, there were only seventeen blockprinters left. Some fabrics were being produced from paper designs taken from old blocks, and it was decided to record all the Liberty block designs on paper to file in the archives with the fabric patterns that go back to the very beginning. Cecil Beaton, when he was costuming *My Fair Lady* in 1960, asked if some fabrics could be printed for him from the original blocks made for *Patience*. The blocks were still there, but not enough men who could hand-print. So they made screens from the blocks and screenprinted the fabrics. Two years later, they started clearing out the thousands of blocks in the block store. One Monday morning Mr Weiner arrived to find a huge quantity piled up outside and, imagining they were going to be burned, he nearly wept. Many were sold to antique dealers, and carried away in lorries. Of the rest, some were sold in the Regent Street shop, some were saved for the archives, and some are treasured by members of the family and Liberty staff.

In 1958 William Poole, assistant to Gustav Weiner, happened on a visit to Paris to find a small exhibition of Art Nouveau. He heard that there was to be another in Amsterdam, and that a much larger Art Nouveau exhibition was planned for June, 1960, at the Museum of Modern Art, New York. He returned to Merton with his fashion antennae twitching and encouraged by Hilary Blackmore and Rosemary Borland, design consultant, started a great search through cupboards full of old swatches of the Art Nouveau period. From amongst them about a dozen furnishing fabrics were chosen that Mr Weiner felt would reproduce well on dress fabrics. Poole re-drew them for silk-screen printing, colouring them in the original shades of the period and also some in brilliant modern colours. They were printed on silk foulard, silk chiffon, wool chiffon and organza; and were named the LOTUS collection after Liberty's first Lotus trade-mark.

The LOTUS collection was shown to the couturiers of London, Paris, and Rome, and was greeted with acclaim – especially by the Romans. The enthusiasm of the Fontana sisters was such that they designed a Lotus Collection of fourteen models within their main collection. Liberty's ordered *toiles* of all fourteen, and also of models in Lotus fabrics by other Roman and Parisian designers, for copying in their own workrooms. The resulting collection was then shown in their Spring 1960 fashion show at Regent Street – a fashion show with a sophistication never seen there before. But the most dramatic appearance of the revived Art Nouveau fabrics was as a climax to the Britannia Ball held at the Astor Hotel, New York. All the members of the Incorporated Society of London Fashion Designers designed models in the Lotus fabrics, and they were worn by the leading London model girls of the day. This event earned for Liberty's 500,000 dollars' worth of free publicity in America, including four colour pages in American *Harper's Bazaar*, two in American *Vogue*, four colour pages in *Look*. Many of the high fashion American ready-to-wear houses ordered Lotus fabrics, and Liberty's exported £78,000 worth to them that first season. Next year there was a strong follow through. Martin Battersby studied the original designs by Bakst for Diaghilev's Russian Ballet and produced six magnificent designs for a BAKST/POIRET range of dress fabrics. These again were ordered by leading New York designers, by the *Haute Couture* of Paris, and the *Alta Moda* of Rome, as also were some original Liberty Paisley designs, re-coloured by William Poole on silk chiffon, foulard, and wool chiffon.

Meanwhile, a fashion revolution was taking place in London. In 1955 Mary Quant opened her first shop called 'Bazaar' in the King's Road, Chelsea. In so doing she lit the fuse to the boutique explosion that was just one of the factors leading up to 'Swinging London' – a term coined by American *Time* magazine in 1964. The 'swinging sixties' have been chronicled by many journalists, and in the ghosted recollections of the leaders of the new society: photographers, model girls, dress designers, hairdressers, group musicians and pop singers. Here it is only relevant to note the stance taken by Liberty's in a London of mini-skirts and short-shift values – with Carnaby Street and its unisex boutiques blaring out discothèque music only just out of earshot. Up Foubert's Place alongside East India House trailed the tourists for whom Carnaby Street had become a more compulsive place to visit than the Tower of London, and for whom the pantomime of London's long-haired youths and mini-skirted maidens provided a fascinating contrast to the Changing of the Guard at Buckingham Palace.

Most of the great department stores felt they must swing with this tide, and opened up 'young boutiques' with cheap and 'trendy' clothes. This Liberty's did not do. Ignoring the more extreme elements of the kinky and the kooky, the pop, the mod, the way-out, spurning the sheer shoddiness of so much of the 'youth-kick' boutiquerie, they introduced clothes designed by the more talented and professional of the young designers who, some of them straight from the Royal College of Art, were making London fashion talked about even in Paris. And with an arrogant high-fashion gesture towards their 'jet set' customers, Liberty's became the exclusive European stockists for Bonnie Cashin of New York. Her clothes, of enormous panache, prestige, and price, have such individual style that elegant consmopolitans buy them as 'classics' – or, to pick up the old Liberty phrase, as 'clothes never out of fashion'.

William Poole left Liberty's at the end of 1962 to take up an appointment in the USA, and his place as fabric designer and colour design consultant was taken by Bernard Nevill, a designer acutely aware of the *zeitgeist*. Just as Poole's fashion antennae had twitched when he heard of the Art Nouveau exhibition to be held in New York in 1960, Nevill's nerve ends responded when he heard there was to be an exhibition of *Les Années Vingt Cinq* at the *Musée des Arts Décoratifs* in Paris in 1966. Art Deco would be in the air. He studied the work of the Omega Workshops, of the Cubists, the Vorticists, the Modernists, the illustrations of Lepape, Marty, and Iribe, the costume and stage designs of Erté, the original 1925 fabric designs of Sonia Delaunay which Zika Ascher was preparing to re-issue. And in the Spring of 1966, the year of the *Années Vingt Cinq* exhibition, Nevill steered a collection of fabrics named JAZZ through the management hierarchy – or perhaps one should say blasted it through. He took the collection to New York, and the influential and ruthless organ of the American garment trade, *Women's Wear Daily*, wrote:

'London began to swing and rock, to go mod, to appear in US headlines as "The Sin Capital of the World". Almost overnight America faced a new London, and concurrently a new LIBERTY, which had picked up the best and re-entered the dance with both feet flying. And one of the men behind the choreography is a groovy young designer Bernard Nevill.'

Thus encouraged, Nevill returned to the Sin Capital of the World and designed another twenties collection, calling it TANGO. And when he took it to New York in June, 1966, *Women's Wear Daily* wrote rapturously of

'Liberty's *enfant terrible*, and his ten-day whirlwind victory over Seventh Avenue . . . thanks to Nevill, Liberty's reputation in America has been revitalised, freed from the stigma of conservatism. Nevill has recalled that Liberty never was merely the bastion of the ancient Paisley and namby-pamby flowered prints, but a unique force in fabric design. Paris, Italy and London have been aware of Liberty's couture range for years. America had lost sight of the fact, but it has re-focussed.' The sights of American fashion reporters are short, considering it was only a few years since their excitement over the LOTUS. and BAKST/POIRET ranges. In dress fabrics, Nevill introduced another kind of twenties feeling with his LANDSCAPE range for 1968: great, flat, horizontal prints of trees and clouds and fields. They were essentially formalised, artificial landscapes – in fact Nevill looked upon this particular exercise as 'a retreat into artificiality'.

In October, 1969, the Sadler's Wells Opera Company revived *Patience* at the London Coliseum. The costumes were designed by John Stoddart and, as in the original production of 1881, Liberty fabrics were used. These were also displayed in an exhibition held concurrently at the National Portrait Gallery called *Patience and the Aesthetes*. It cannot be said that this revival of *Patience* brought about a revival of the Aesthetic Movement; but it was surely not entirely coincidental that it took place at a time when fashion reporters had started writing about a Pre-Raphaelite vogue, and photographers began to tell their model girls to look pale and sorrowful. Shop-figures also, which through the sixties had been modelled in defiant attitudes with legs astride, were thrown on the scrap-heap in favour of poetic figures sculpted in drooping poses and given Pre-Raphaelite hair styles. There was a revival of tie-and-dye fabrics, mostly perpetrated by amateurs, and a variety of vaguely ethnic fashions. The most bizarre manifestation of aesthetic attire were the 'hippies', trailing around the streets in pavement-length skirts, droopy shawls, tatty blouses, tangled hair. But their philosophy did not seem to be so much 'art for art's sake' as tat for tat's sake. There were, however, just a few London designers – Thea Porter, Zandra Rhodes, Bill Gibb – who were creating very expensive, timeless and totally irrelevant dresses which could only be justified as art for art's sake, fantasies conjured up with brocades and embroideries, beading, ribbons, feathers, satins, frail chiffons, and some of Liberty's most unashamedly extravagant fabrics.

Bernard Nevill had sensed the approach of this reaction from the ultra-short, geometrically constructed clothes in firm gaberdine and other plain fabrics that had obtained since Courrèges's 'Space Age' collection of 1964; and he was ready in that Autumn of the *Patience* revival with a RENAISSANCE range of damask weave tapestry patterns converted into prints on very fine wool challis. Yves Saint Laurent chose many of these for the collection in which he dropped his skirt length to mid-calf; and he asked Nevill to design an exclusive range of prints on cotton for his next Spring collection of ready-to-wear Rive Gauche clothes. This was the beginning of Liberty's trade with the French *prêt-à-porter* which, under the guidance of the redoubtable Gilbert Saada (now a director of Liberty & Co.) has extended ever since. It is not only the new ranges that the *prêt-à-porter* orders. Thousands of yards of the 'little florals' on Tana Lawn are used each season by French houses such as Cacharel and Daniel Hechter. And when in 1970 Ungaro started the fashion for using different types of pattern in one outfit, Liberty brought out a CHAMELEON range of stripes, chevrons, diagonals, and chessboard squares, all linked by the same colour philosophy and all capable of being mixed together.

That was Bernard Nevill's last range for Liberty's, and in 1972 Susan Collier was appointed. There was a feeling for the thirties in the air, so she produced a FAUVISTE range of dress fabrics, and her furnishing ranges included some startlingly aggressive designs inspired by the Bauhaus as well as other more traditional designs. She feels timing is all important . . . 'Eyes become accustomed to adventurous new designs if a few are brought in each season.' She pays tribute to Blair Pride, the Liberty producer, who died tragically young after eleven years with the firm . . . 'It was he who taught me what Liberty's was about; he was the holder of the Liberty conscience. He got the best out of the designer, the best out of the colourists, the screen makers and the printers.' Susan Collier visited the widow of Claud Lovat Fraser, whose recollections of being bought clothes at Liberty's when a child are quoted in Chapter 8. Together they went through the original Lovat Fraser designs for *The Beggar's Opera* and other stage productions, also the textiles he originally designed for Foxton, some of which were probably bought by Liberty's. From this wealth of inspiration, Susan Collier created a LOVAT FRASER range of dress fabrics. That same season, some of the designs originally bought by Liberty from the Silver Studio were re-issued on Country Cotton; while Susan Collier and her Studio contributed, and continue to contribute, hundreds of original designs for the Liberty bank.

During the whole post-war renaissance period, the designers and design editors have been backed up at Merton by Liberty of London Prints' own studio of skilled colourists, and in the Regent Street shop by the buyers and managers forming Mr C. L. Roth's strong team. To name them all would make too long a list. But their enthusiasm, acumen and expertise have been essential elements in the revitalising of the Liberty image.

The Oriental Department benefited during the 1960s by a general fashion for party clothes of Eastern inspiration – principally caftans, but also tunic and trouser suits, quilted Maharajah coats, embroidered slippers and evening bags, long Indian scarves. In 1970, Henry Rothschild undertook a special Indian journey for his own shop Primavera, and for Liberty's. He returned with treasure trove worthy of the great days of merchant adventuring . . . hand-woven brocades from Jaipur and Benares; block-printed silks embroidered with gold and silver; tie-dyed cottons and silks, gorgeous saris. There were 'curios' from theatres, temples, and remote villages, carvings from Madras and Andra Pradesh, Bidri work-boxes, masks, and a collection of rare jewellery. More recently, Richard Stewart-Liberty, great-nephew of the Founder, made a journey to China with Miss Rosalind Christie, buyer of the Jewellery Department, travelling wherever they were allowed, searching for original hand-made pieces. In the same year his brother Oliver, in his capacity as sales manager of Liberty of London Prints Ltd, travelled through France, Italy, the USA, Canada, and Japan.

In 1973 Liberty's acquired the famous firm of Metz and Co. (founded in 1740), with shops at Amsterdam, The Hague, and Schipol Airport. Metz had sold Liberty fabrics since 1898, and in 1902 became sole Liberty agents in Holland with a complete department for Liberty specialities. They issued Metz-Liberty catalogues, and the second name of Metz rapidly became Liberty, even appearing on their delivery vans. Joseph de Leeuw, director and owner of Metz at that time, was a great admirer of Liberty's of London, and this influenced the way in which he conducted his business. He was a man of taste and interests very similar to those of Arthur Lasenby Liberty; and like him he had close contacts and friendships with designers, artists and architects. Through these contacts, Metz became the leading store in Holland for modern furniture. Joseph de Leeuw died in a German concentration camp in 1944, and his son Hendrik de Leeuw, who had trained at Liberty's in the 1920s, took over the business in 1945. He is now coming up to retirement age, and since his son has chosen a career in music, he decided to offer Metz to Liberty & Co. His management and staff were all agreed that Liberty's were the only firm in the world with which they would happily merge. The long friendship has ended in marriage.

Unlike the biography of a famous person, the biography of this famous shop cannot be brought to a neat conclusion with the subject's death. It could have been brought to a fine conflagration if the IRA fire-bombs planted in the store in August 1973 had not been detected. As it is, the story must remain open-ended. Nevertheless, there is a romantic rightness that it has in so many ways, at the close of these first hundred years, come full circle. Arthur Liberty's descendants and other emissaries are now, as in the beginning, exploring the Orient for its carpets, its fabrics and embroideries, its ceramics, its jewellery and jade. The long love affair with the Americans is still warm. In this present generation there are many who, like the Bohemians of Arthur Liberty's young days, like to wear what they please, including 'costumes never out of fashion'. Present taste is tending again towards gentler colours, softer outlines, to shapes that beguile the senses – the word aesthetic is with us again, and quality has its connoisseurs. Although there is not yet another Maison Liberty in Paris, Liberty's have returned to Europe via Holland; and just as the influential Paul Poiret used Liberty fabrics, so does the most influential of modern couturiers, Yves Saint Laurent. And there is yet one more most satisfying full circle – Liberty fabrics are now exported to Japan, from whence Arthur Liberty imported the first oriental silks for his first half-shop in Regent Street.

Rossetti, having just had a fresh consignment of 'stunning' fabrics from that new shop in Regent Street, tries hard to prevail on his younger sister to accept at any rate one of these and have a dress made of it from designs to be furnished by himself.

'What *is* the use, Christina, of having a heart like a singing bird and a water-shoot and all the rest of it, if you insist on getting yourself up like a pew-opener?'

By Max Beerbohm, from *Rossetti and His Circle*, published by William Heinemann Ltd. Reproduced by courtesy of the Trustees of the Tate Gallery

Stag design by C. F. A. Voysey, 1896. Originally designed as a wallpaper, and subsequently woven by Alexander Morton & Co. for Liberty furnishing fabric

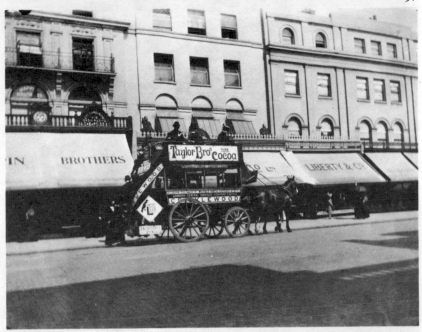

East India House, Regent Street, late 1890s

Maison Liberty, 38 avenue de l'Opéra, Paris, 1889

Indian print scarf

Indian ring-stripe design

Opposite: Japanese wood-cut design on silk, *c.* 1880

By Lindsay P. Butterfield. Printed for Liberty's by G. P. &
J. Baker, *c.* 1900

Couture salon of the Maison Liberty, 3 boulevard des Capucines

Madame Poiret on Paul Poiret's yacht, 1909; wearing 'Carotte', made in a Liberty fabric, many coloured design dominated by carrot red. Photograph by courtesy of Madame Poiret. From *Poiret* by Palmer White, published by Studio Vista

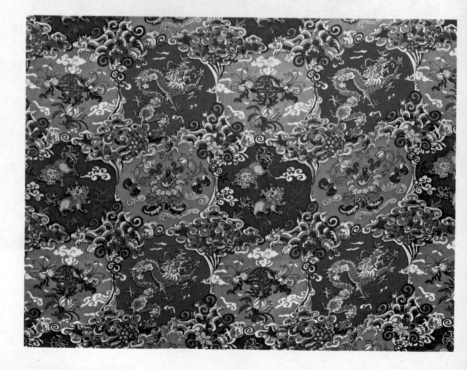

Tana Lawn, *c.* 1930

Opposite: Traditional Indian shawl design, used for a shawl of the 1930s

Dog and Dragon design. Liberty block print based on a Chinese design, *c.* 1900. Still in use converted to screen printing

Tana Lawn by Blair Pride, *c.* 1960

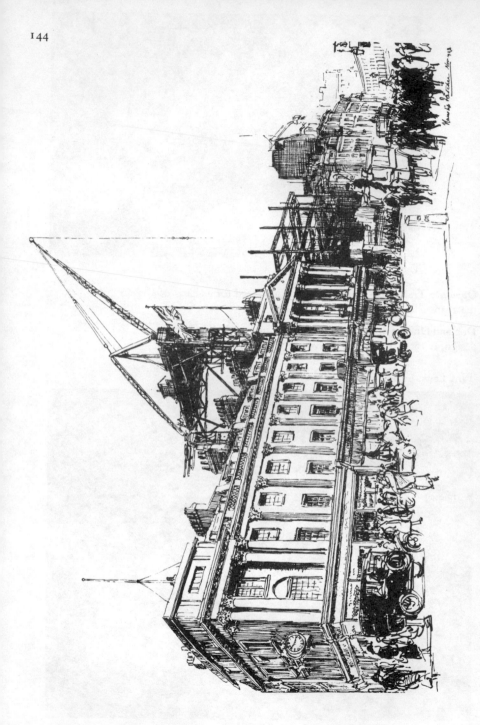

The Last of Chesham House. Pen and ink by Hanslip Fletcher

Liberty's Tudor Building. Pen and ink by Hanslip Fletcher

Art Nouveau furnishing fabric, designed for Liberty by Harry Napper, 1900

Art Nouveau furnishing fabric, designed for Liberty by J. Scarrett Rigby, 1897

Empire gown 'Josephine' and Art Nouveau furnishings, Liberty 'Dress and Decoration' catalogue, *c.* 1905

Scheme for a diningroom, drawn by A. M. Lewis of Liberty's Contracts
Department for a client in Cape Town, c. 1930

East India House, Regent Street, after the rebuilding, 1927

Dinner gown in Dalghali silk-crepe; Spring catalogue, 1915

The Lotus Collection of revived Art Nouveau fabrics, 1960. Dresses by the
leading London couture designers worn by the top model girls of the period,
in the Crush Bar at the Royal Opera House. Photograph in the possession of
William Poole

Oriental Carpet Department, late 1920s. Note rugs hung over the gallery

Arthur I. Stewart-Liberty, the present Chairman

Ivor Stewart-Liberty, Chairman, 1930–2

From Martin Battersby's Bakst/Poiret designs, 1961
From Bernard Nevill's 'Renaissance' range, 1969

Susan Collier's furnishing fabric 'Splendide', for the Centenary Collection, 1975

Susan Collier's 'Bauhaus' from her Clarion Collection of furnishing fabrics, 1972

Mary Quant dress in Liberty print, 1970. Exhibited at the 'Mary Quant's London' exhibition, London Museum, November 1973–June 1974

From Yves Saint Laurent's Rive Gauche Collection, Automne-Hiver, 1969–70. Kilt in Liberty Varuna wool, Nevill's 'Macedonia' design.

Liberty's come full circle in Centenary year, with a 1975 kimono dress designed by Lily Henkit of Holland in Lantana flower print by Susan Collier

INDEX

Italic figures denote illustrations